MW00653754

Reclaiming PROPHECY

Encouraging Church Leaders to Rethink Prophetic Ministry

By Darin Slack

Copyright © 2015 by Darin Slack

All rights reserved. No part of this book may be used, reproduced, stored in a retrieval system, or transmitted in any form whatsoever — including electronic, photocopy, recording — without prior written permission from the author, except in the case of brief quotations embodied in critical articles or reviews.

Unless otherwise indicated, all scripture quotations are from *The Holy Bible, English Standard Version*® (ESV®). Copyright ©2001 by Crossway Bibles, a division of Good News Publishers. Used by permission. All rights reserved.

FIRST EDITION

ISBN: 978-0-9962716-2-2

Library of Congress Control Number: 2015938551

Published by

P.O. Box 2839, Apopka, FL 32704

Printed in the United States of America

Disclaimer: The views and opinions expressed in this book are solely those of the authors and other contributors. These views and opinions do not necessarily represent those of Certa Publishing.

For Jesus, My Prophet, and My Savior

Table of Contents

Part 1: The Mission of Prophecy
DIRECTION - Why do we have the gifts and what is their goal?
DISTINCTION - What are the different gifts?

Part 2: The Models of Prophecy
DISCERNMENT - Where is the pastor's and church's current
level of faith for the gifts and manifestations of the Spirit?

Part 3: The Messengers of Prophecy
DISCIPLESHIP - Who are we training in the
prophetic ministry and how?

Part 4: The Ministry of Prophecy
DEVELOPMENT - How are we going to grow
the gift in our local church?

Foreword

Prophecy...

Dear pastor, co-laborer, friend,

Where would you be personally in the continuum between "eagerly desiring" prophecy and being "open but cautious?" I can understand any hesitation you may have, even angst, when it comes to discerning how the more public or vocal gifts of the Spirit "fit in" to the "normal" day-to-day life of the local church.

Honestly, it's messy.

We see evidence of that in the church at Corinth and we've seen it in our own church for the last thirty years!

When we began in 1984, our idealistic and passionate pursuit of all God had for us in the church today drove us to ask of the Lord a daring question: What would be His pleasure regarding prophecy for our mission as a church? We were asking the same thing for every other aspect of our life together so we couldn't, in good conscience, ignore this one part of what we see so clearly in Scripture.

Not to say that the other areas of our mission were easy, but this one seemed to stir up a wide variety of problems that, at times, seemed insurmountable.

It was certainly frustrating for me as a senior pastor, but I can only imagine how difficult it was for those in the church gifted in prophecy! We would challenge our church members to serve with the gifts God had given them, but when our folks who had the gift of prophecy tried to serve, it proved...troublesome.

As a pastor, trying to lead well, many times I felt like I was "in the way" much more than I was a part of the answer.

All that is in hindsight now, and for that I am thankful! After three decades, and the patience that only the Holy Spirit can provide, we have come to a place in our church where these gifts are flourishing like never before. We haven't arrived and figured it all out by any means. Over these years together, there have been many wonderful seasons of blessing, and much fruit has been born as a result. But the love, faithfulness, endurance, long-suffering, and passion for all God has for us has sustained the pastoral leadership of the church, as well as those who have been given this wonderful gift.

What Darin has prepared for you here is a feast! It's all your favorite foods, even things you wouldn't have thought to ask for. He is sharing honestly our successes and failures. He is taking you down the path we traveled.

And why? Oh how we would have loved to have had a resource like this on our journey! At least we could have gleaned from others and learned from their experience. During our quest, we found very little that was published to help us. Darin earnestly desires to change that and make available to you all that we've learned so that you can get from where you are now to where you want to be.

This book is an answer to innumerable prayers. It is a dream come true for me and for Darin. It is our sincere prayer that you will benefit and grow in this spiritual gift and the wonderful expression of the Holy Spirit's activity it is in the life of the local church.

Danny Jones
Pastor, Metro Life Church
Orlando, Florida
March 11, 2015

Preface

Wherever you declare yourself along the spectrum of belief about prophetic ministry, I believe your curiosity in this title is not by chance.

And I realize the difficulty for leaders to corral such a powerful—and potentially scary—gift, but I also believe God still redeems what has been lost.

This book exists because many Christian leaders are discarding a critical grace gift to the church—*prophecy*. The volatile, divisive, and noxious fumes of past abuse and misuse still linger in the atmosphere of many churches. This has left many leaders with no choice but to deny or marginalize the gift.

Have you ever considered the possibility that the enemy has sought to minimize, abuse, and counterfeit this gift of prophecy above all the others because the Apostle Paul, writing by the Holy Spirit, singled it out for its potential to strengthen and edify the Church more than all the others?

When I shared this burden and early manuscript with my pastors, they encouraged me to move forward because while they had read books on prophecy, they had never read one like mine. In essence they said, "This book hasn't been written, not in this way and not to us—to leaders."

This is not about promoting an experience or "building brands." It's about understanding and embracing the inestimable value of having "ears to hear" what the Spirit is saying to the Church through the grace of a much maligned and misunderstood gift.

I'm not going to make a defense of the gift; that's a well-traveled road by many excellent scholars. Nor am I going to sit in judgment on ministries claiming prophetic anointing. Instead, I'd like to offer a perspective. More specifically, a process.

With thirty years of submitted local church prophetic ministry and insight into the missteps and successes, I've distilled into five steps the milestones of the Holy Spirit's faithful work in maturing this gift in me and in my local church. I will walk you through *DIRECTION, DISTINCTION, DISCERNMENT, DISCIPLESHIP,* and *DEVELOPMENT* to train those gifted in prophecy in your churches to serve the Body of Christ.

I hope to re-envision the hearts of leaders and laity alike for a gift that Paul declared should be foremost in our desires for the Holy Spirit's manifestations.

Following the Apostle Paul's Corinthian example of not calling for the eradication of prophecy because of error, abuse, and failure, I want to encourage, as he did, the priority of prophecy while offering a biblically sound, administratively practical point of view on its managed integration, operation, and growth in the local church.

It's my prayer that this gospel-centered, God-focused content will be a catalyst to *reclaim* the gift of prophecy and the Holy Spirit's purpose for it in your life and local church.

May it inspire a fresh discussion and demonstration of the unchanged command of the Holy Spirit in 1 Corinthians 14:1 (emphasis added): "Pursue love, and earnestly desire spiritual gifts, *especially that you may prophesy.*"

It's my passion to see the glorious Church of Jesus Christ equipped and matured in this gift ministry and God's immutable grace.

Darin Slack

Part 1: The Mission of Prophecy

Introduction to Part 1

*DIRECTION - Why do we have the gifts and
what is their goal in the local church?*

*DISTINCTION - What are the
differences between the gifts?*

In order to manage growth of any kind, there must be a process. As leaders, we must lean on the Holy Spirit to provide insight and wisdom to understand where the church has been, know where it currently abides, and have faith for where we need to lead it. I've sought to interweave the 5-step process of growing prophetic ministry (*DIRECTION, DISTINCTION, DISCERNMENT, DISCIPLESHIP, and DEVELOPMENT*) with each part of this book to simplify and manage expectations.

This first section will provide a biblical *DIRECTION,* or *mission,* for us to pursue, and along the way, we hope to make some key *DISTINCTIONS* that are designed to overcome objections and issues that arise when talking about this gift and its administration in the mission of prophecy.

Chapter 1

Prophecy in the New Testament Church Is a "Thing"

"Pursue love, and eagerly desire the spiritual gifts, especially that you may prophesy." (1 Cor. 14:1)

"For you can all prophesy, one by one, that all may learn and all be encouraged." (1 Cor. 14:31)

"So, my brothers, earnestly desire to prophesy, and do not forbid speaking in tongues." (1 Cor. 14:39)

Do you eagerly desire spiritual gifts in your walk with Christ? In your church? Is prophecy at the top of that list? Scripture says it's for each believer indwelt by the Holy Spirit, something we can learn, and something we can be encouraged by. It's my passion to see leaders and believers in the local church learn this ministry and be encouraged to obey God in its use.

There will be no effort to defend these Scriptures. There is no need. Each pastor who has the Spirit knows by his spirit what these verses are saying.

Do you hear the voice of God in your life, and do you share what you hear with others?

You may call it what you want, an impression, a prodding or a quickening, but the Holy Spirit, by the hand of Paul, calls this manifestation "prophecy." If we claim to want all God has for us and our church—what His Scripture commands—then we simply must eagerly desire to prophesy.

When we get comfortable with the idea that the Spirit no longer manifests the gift of prophecy, He sends someone to us speaking about things in our life and church they could never know, which quietly leaves us stunned and yearning for more of what we don't really understand.

Or, we have a dream so vivid in clarity and scope, we awaken with an imprinted memory so real, it's as if we were actually there. Though we may have no idea what it means, we know only the Spirit could have drawn so great a picture and we want more.

Or, our prayer and study is suddenly interrupted by a powerful rush of voice and vision from within us so that we are reduced to sobbing tears. The peace is so deep we can find no words, only a wrenching longing to know the Spirit drawing us closer.

Heaven invades our intellect in these moments. Like a wrecking ball through an old building, our simple grasp of God is literally shattered to dust. We are ruined, yet so deeply in love with Him. We are broken, yet so captivated by His grace. The God who flung the stars and spread out the universe, the Ancient One, Faithful and True, the Delight of all Heaven and the human heart, has spoken. And we heard it; somehow, we know it.

There is no cessationism, no critique, and no argument in that moment with the Spirit. Like Paul, we can only say, "Who are you, Lord?" Some even may experience conviction, as Paul did, to consider how we may be persecuting the Holy Spirit in our hearts, teaching, and critique or avoidance of His work.

We could realize in these solemn moments that we are at risk of being like John in Mark 9:38, who tried to stop anyone who walked with Jesus who wasn't exactly like the disciples.

> John said to him, "Teacher, we saw someone casting out demons in your name, and we tried to stop him, because he was not following us." But Jesus said,

"Do not stop him, for no one who does a mighty work
in my name will be able soon afterward to speak evil
of me. For the one who is not against us is for us."
(Mark 9:38-40)

The ones who do mighty works in Jesus' name, including
what we don't fully grasp, are with us, even if we aren't with
them or their way of doing it. We must plead with the Spirit to
extract from our heart the Pharisee of Luke 18:10-11 that says,
"I'm glad I'm not like the extortioners, unjust, and adulterers
who exploit the Holy Spirit for personal gain" (paraphrased). We
must ask Him to restore the publican's posture in Luke 18:13, of
standing far off, not lifting our eyes to heaven, and crying out for
mercy for our prejudiced and uncharitable hearts.

May He grant us all the humility that will exalt Him and
build our understanding of His Spirit's work, while He humbles
our exalted critique of what He can and cannot do, will and
will not do, in the midst of the Church. A Church He purchased
at unfathomable expense by the precious blood of Heaven's
dearest, the Savior of our hearts, Jesus Christ.

Pastors recognize their responsibility to God and to their
congregation, but often their preached view of God can come
across in a manner that invites the Spirit to work, but not in every
way Scripture reveals as viable. The Spirit works through people
by granting them "gifts," among them prophecy, an overlooked
and possibly even disturbing manifestation of the Spirit.

Like train tracks parallel to one another, this book's first
track aims to restore a vision for the spiritual gifts, especially the
prophetic, in the heart of the pastor. At the same time, we will
explore a very practical parallel track, hints from Scripture and
personal experience pertaining to the manifestation of the Spirit
prophetically in our everyday lives.

Gifts will flourish in God's Church if leadership is
intentional and full of faith to see them manifested by the Spirit.

Loving one another, living honestly before God, and
studying our Bibles are pastoral messages that will not arrest
passivity in building the Church. There must be a demonstration

of power; the Holy Spirit's transforming, releasing, risk-producing, boldness-building power through the gifts.

Pastors must provide a biblical *Direction* for the spiritual gifts, their place in the Church, and our planned pursuit so faith can grow. They must continue building faith by defining, or *Distinguishing*, the nuanced differences in the ways the gifts manifest, to encourage individuals to see how the Holy Spirit uses them specifically.

They must *Discern* the current level of faith in the church and *Disciple* to equip and build the church to maturity in the administration of the gifts. Finally, they must *Develop* it through training and use.

If we can see the process of *Direction, Distinction, Discernment, Discipleship, and Development* play out in our churches, we would see lives quickly change, revival burst forth, and the gospel usher out in power. It's *not* dependent on our performance, but on our willingness to draw near in faith to what the Spirit of God has *already promised He would do*. Then, and only then, will He do what He wants to do in and through us.

DIRECTION - Why do we have the gifts and what is their goal in the local church?

Chapter 2

Opening the Door to Prophecy

"Just don't leave." These were the words of my pastor, Danny Jones, in the early years at the church I'm still in today.

He wasn't pleading as if God was telling me to leave. He didn't want me to allow criticisms from others to stifle the young prophetic gift I displayed or to make me run away out of fear or frustration.

I had been led by the Spirit of God to this church out of a prominent charismatic fellowship, which at the time was a severe reverse culture shock. My new church was much more conservative on everything, including the gifts.

Prophecy wasn't a new thing to them, and the leadership encouraged the gift's use. They even had prophetic ministers come in and minister to the church. But clearly, care, character, and doctrinal preaching were the only real focus.

What's wrong with that? Raise that question in a room full of pastors and there will be amens and affirmation all around.

Except we know from Scripture that the Church doesn't primarily exist to be cared for, have great character, and to be preached to by pastors who love to speak; pastors are called to equip, build up, and make disciples in the Church--disciples who preach the true gospel of Jesus Christ to a lost and dying world, with a demonstration of the Holy Spirit's power that produces lasting change for the glory of God.

We aren't called to setup a meeting where everyone's felt-needs are met, everyone gets to see their friends and to fellowship, and everyone learns a Sunday school lesson that really hits us in the heart. That is a club with a motivational speaker. That is not the *ekklesia*, the "called out" ones, the Church of Jesus Christ, currently engaged in a holy war.

Believers certainly need care, character, and preaching, but we are foremost children of the most High God, who need the manifest power of the Holy Spirit every moment of every day.

The call to war against materialism, idolatry, and secret sin can too easily become the focus of our weekly meetings. Personal holiness is important, but rooting out personal failure can easily displace the burning passion for fulfilling God's calling to go forth in His great power!

When the Holy Spirit uses us to manifest His love and glory, we are compelled to live rightly by the grace of God that teaches us to say no to ungodliness (Titus 2). But if we only hear what we need to work on in ourselves, no matter how much grace is preached with it, we lose heart.

Most pastors truly desire power for Christ-glorifying ministry through the Holy Spirit in their ministry. They must equally pray the same for the gifts resident in their congregation or they can grow complacent and comfortable. In the members' minds, it can appear easier and safer to leave all ministry to the pastor. Pastors wondering why they have such a "quiet" and unresponsive congregation may not realize that their significant efforts to care, build character, and preach doctrine has unwittingly led their congregation to an anemic "spectator" mentality.

Paul said in 1 Corinthians 2:3-5 (NIV, emphasis added),

I came to you in weakness with great fear and trembling. My message and my preaching were not with wise and persuasive words, **but with a demonstration of the Spirit's power**, so that your faith might not rest on human wisdom, but on God's power.

Many pastors quietly assent that the charismatic gifts (prophecy for our purposes) continued after the first-century Church. Called *continuationists* today, but not fully associating with charismatic culture, they identify with the gifts as continuing in principle, but they do so "under protest." They are likely protesting unrestrained, unaccountable, uncontrolled ministry they see or fear.

Like many on the fringes of the faith who want Jesus but not the Church, they want the Holy Spirit, just not as He's being portrayed by those who claim to have Him. They may genuinely want to see most of the gifts in action, but aspects of the charismatic culture appears so "anti-order" to them that managing prophetic people who would come in with controversial gifts and might immediately criticize their doctrine, refuse to play by the "rules," and/or not appreciate what elders face in cleaning up after them, is simply not worth the risk.

Those who pursue some gifts may lay down so many disclaimers and cautions about the gifts of the Holy Spirit that they default to functional cessationism because they have yet to see a model of truly gifted, accountable, Holy Spirit-empowered prophetic ministry they can support. This doesn't mean these prophetic people don't exist; they just haven't met them yet.

Other pastors fall into another category of having tried the "gift experiment," only to fail in some way. It became too much to administrate, it got out of control, took the focus away from more important things, or didn't bear lasting fruit. Also, they may not have had anyone who could help them administrate it. They didn't have a proven prophet or see anyone with a level of maturity in their gifting and doctrine who could help equip and train the gift ministries.

Another common occurrence is the pastor who invites a visiting prophet who didn't come to help others be equipped for ministry, but came to minister. Response to such a prophet may be strong, but the church still needs to grow its own prophetic ministry. The visiting prophet, like pastors who only preach and do not equip in gifts, creates a "spectator spirit" that makes the congregation content to watch and not participate.

Still other pastors may be comfortable with a certain measure of spiritual gift development and inclusion in the corporate gathering, but don't know how to create a strategic plan to develop people in their gifts and callings.

Here's a way to sum up what I believe to be the challenges facing pastors.

In addition to caring, building character, and preaching, all pastors know they are to prayerfully identify, develop, equip, and mature gift ministries within the Church themselves. It's part of their Ephesians 4 call to equip and build the Church to fulfill its various callings. But, truthfully, many aren't even sure what those relationships with Ephesians 4 gift ministries is supposed to look like, much less work together to build the Church.

Many conclude that the apostle and prophet must have ceased in the first century. Where are the examples of gifted believers? The few in the public eye are solo evangelists and prophets, and if they are busy building their own "brands," then the pastor is left holding down the local church alone. So they wait.

Pastors are on the tip of the spear fighting for the people of God every day, holding whatever ground they've captured, only to have to deal with believers practicing the gifts who aren't partners in building the local church, but people who need more leadership than the pastor feels he has to give.

Instead of the gift ministries arriving to serve the pastors in the local church, they come in expecting to out-rank them and be served for their anointing. These unchecked gift ministries lack validating qualities the pastor needs to see, like humility, genuine care for the local church, observable character, and sound doctrinal preaching that equips, not entertains.

No wonder pastors are fearful and fatigued!

I believe the Holy Spirit is doing a new work to counteract the undisciplined and immature prophet and the brand-building soloists out there.

I believe he's going to envision pastors everywhere to engage the gifts in their local churches.

I was one of those immature and exhausting prophets, but

God has been faithful to give me local pastors who recognized my calling as a partner with a slightly different function - to provide the same care, character, and sound doctrine in the equipping of the gifts. Together, we have stumbled along, guided by faith, to discover a clear, God-given vision for the gifts.

Pastors will have to open their hearts to the Holy Spirit giving gifts, coming alongside manifesting believers to equip the saints for the work of ministry.

It's my hope that what He's taught us will inspire pastors to open the door to the gifts again, with fresh vision that we may prophesy.

My Introduction to the Voice of God

I first encountered Jesus in my early days of college. God grew me as a leader in many ways – in on-campus ministry, in church, and among a secular crowd. I became an All-American college quarterback, who led others, while God was constructing a plan to humble me greatly so He could use me.

The early days of my Christian faith were filled with the presence of the Holy Spirit. I didn't understand what it was at the time; I just felt like I was being followed everywhere. At times, I literally had to stop and look around to see if anyone was there.

He was there. Just beyond the veil of the world I could see, He was holding me close like a Father who couldn't stop hugging a wayward son who'd returned after being gone for a long time. I was being loved by Him.

And His voice, oh, His voice was magnificent in my spirit.

When I heard it for the first time, I was shocked by the clarity and majesty of it invading my entire being. During the first week after my conversion, I encountered a difficult situation and was questioning His character and sovereignty in my heart. I certainly never expected Him to answer, but He did in what I can only describe as a deep impression upon my soul that was both patient and profound.

It wasn't audible, or accompanied by lightning and

thunder, but it had that effect. It was unexpected, unforgettable and unmistakable. I was blown away.

Imagine a deaf person hearing sound for the first time. That's what it was to hear God speak for the first time. It was so matter-of-fact, yet so different than my normal thoughts, so strong in its conviction, yet so incredibly kind. I was captivated by His voice.

I suddenly understood Elijah's reaction when he didn't respond to the earthquake and fire God had sent him, but Elijah exploded out of his self-absorbed state when he heard the "still small voice" saying, "Why are you here?" (1 Kings 19:12-13).

I had heard the "still small voice." It might have been still, or quiet, but to me, it certainly wasn't small.

I heard His voice not with my ears, but rather my heart. It appears mad and marvelous at the same time. His words paint pictures of peace and calm on the canvas of my mind. His voice stimulates my emotion, intellect, and will, all at once, as if they rise in honor of who is speaking. Even before my conscious mind can catch up to what happened, I know what He said. How I know is unexplainable, but the clarity is unmistakable and the conviction it produces is palpable.

I've since grown to understand the nuances in His tone as well. If it's a call to obedience, my busy thoughts are silenced, and I am lost in the fulfillment of His word. If it's an affirmation, it empties all my ambition and bids me toss the glory at His feet. If it's a correction, my soul is arrested, and His mercy floods my failure. No matter what direction His voice takes in me, I cannot stay the same when I hear Him.

At times, His voice can be so quiet and so considerate that I will dismiss it out of hand. To my shame and utter foolishness, I believe the kind and wise thought my own, rather than give glory to whom it's due.

We must never become so accustomed to God speaking to us that we diminish one moment of that wonderful expression of His grace.

To hear His voice is among the ultimate privileges purchased by Christ in our inheritance as the children of God. He paid an incalculable debt we could not pay, bridged a distance we could not measure, and plumbed a depth we could not fathom.

Scripture and the Voice of God

There is no competition between the supremacy of Scripture and God's voice. His Spirit dwells in me, and speaks to me the unchanging truths of Scripture, which etch their way deeper and deeper into my unsanctified mind.

Though I have an imperfect mind and a corrupt temptation to sin, I am still bid to interpret His voice. That makes Scripture the greatest tool with the highest authority to confirm what I believe I hear from Him. There will be no conflict. However, as I listen more and more, the Holy Spirit takes Scripture and applies it to my life, identifies my heart in it, and edifies me with it. He echoes its essence in my heart and mind and is always making more of Jesus in me with it every day of my life. He speaks plainly, not always in verse, but never in contradiction to Scripture, and always directing me deeper in it.

The voice of God is, and always has been, speaking to men's lost hearts, from the beginning of time when He called out in the garden, "Adam, where are you?" He draws men to Himself, reveals Himself to them, and transforms them by His Spirit.

The Essence of Prophetic Ministry:
Bringing the Eternal into the Temporal

I have walked in the Holy Spirit for many years; I have seen many different prophetic manifestations. Regardless of content or style, one thing that has remained constant in my own prophetic experience is an unrelenting sense of urgency from the Spirit regarding His love for the gathered people of God.

He absolutely and unreservedly loves His people, and He enthusiastically reminds me of that every time I ask how I can serve them. Like I didn't hear Him the first time, He recounts for me His undying passion for His saints. His energetic anticipation of any setting where He intends to bless His gathered people is the first thing I prophetically sense. I do not possess that care and compassion for His people on my own; therefore it is an excellent way to confirm I'm hearing God—if I feel greater love for His people than I am capable of, it's God.

True prophetic ministry exists to trumpet His deep affection for His Church. Like the groom declaring over and over his unswerving devotion to his bride in preparation for their wedding, we must meet each moment of His compassion through the prophetic as if it were the first time.

There is no way to exhaust the love of God for His Church prophetically. We will run out of breath to speak long before He tires one iota of telling the Church how much He loves her.

Every true anointed prophetic moment has been saturated in power that opens my eyes to the depth of His love for His people. Even in Jesus' most stinging rebuke of the Pharisees, you hear His love pouring forth, "Jerusalem, Jerusalem, you who kill the prophets and stone those sent to you, how often I have longed to gather your children together, as a hen gathers her chicks under her wings, and you were not willing" (Matt. 23:37 NIV).

The Church needs to be regularly reminded of Christ's unchanging love, as we are prone to drift away in busyness, idolatry, and the cares of life. At times, we are stubborn, unwilling children who must be brought back by the overwhelming kindness of the Father. Jesus took upon Himself the lethal rebuke of God's wrath we fully deserved for our sin, and He has forever removed any condemnation in the Father's voice toward us (Rom. 8:1).

The Father's Voice Always Sounds of Pure, Unreserved Kindness

In the Old Testament, prophets often took a harsh tone (coupled with the most tender expressions of compassion you'll ever hear). Before the cross, God's Wrath had not been satisfied. Today, after the work of the cross, there should never be a harsh tone in true prophetic ministry. Because of Christ, condemnation has been completely eradicated and all we should hear in the Father's voice is kindness that leads us to repentance.

Any harsh assessment of the Church and her obvious weakness is flawed and self-righteous. We should be regularly and wonderfully swept up in the new mercies of God pouring forth from the gospel of prophetic anointing.

This doesn't mean we never address sin, but a harsh prophetical tone for the Church is from our uncharitable and impatient hearts. But God is charity and patience personified; should we grow harsh, He will patiently lift our eyes to see what He sees—not a flawed people as they now are, but as the faithful people they will become by His grace, a glorious and unified Church!

Through anointed prophetic ministry, He's going to use His eternal perspective of our glorious future to wash away the temporal perspective of our circumstance and failures that steal our joy.

This is the essence of prophetic ministry—to continually, through His unimaginable kindness, redirect the Church's temporal perspective toward the eternal.

Why Do Spiritual Gifts, Especially Prophecy, Matter?

The gifts mentioned in Scripture, especially prophecy, exist as manifestations of the indwelling Holy Spirit to herald the heart of God among His people in the most intimate way possible, meeting our deepest needs, and speaking to our deepest selves about who He is in our lives.

The Holy Spirit is manifesting the grace of Jesus Christ through the gifts. The point is never to make much of the spiritual gifts, but of Jesus. That is what the Holy Spirit was sent to do, and the gifts are a means of grace to make it so. If we hope to see the gifts manifesting in our meetings, then we have to make room for the Holy Spirit to lead and participate.

We must not just assume that He wishes to bless our plan to glorify God, but that He wishes to glorify Jesus through us in His chosen way, through our faith.

The gifts function by faith in God, but they also increase faith when they are manifested. Faith that must continue to grow, so we see these gifts, especially prophecy, become a great and powerful demonstration of His love and power to a lost and dying world, through us, His Church. "For it is the Spirit of prophecy who bears testimony to Jesus" (Rev. 19:10b NIV).

Jesus is the reason we have gifts and are using them for His glory. This is entirely about Him. When the gifts manifest, they should unswervingly point to the grace and mercy of Jesus Christ in our midst. The Holy Spirit was sent for that purpose, and any demonstration of power, especially prophecy, that does not point us to Jesus Christ alone, is not of Him and should be avoided.

We must demystify the gifts by seeing them for what they are. They are Holy Spirit expressions of God's mercy, grace, and love toward us, and through us, at the point of our deepest need. They are made possible through the finished work of Jesus Christ on the cross and His resurrection from the dead. To suggest that they exist for any other purpose than to make much of Jesus is to make much of ourselves.

Chapter 3

Two Purposes of New Testament Prophecy

1) To Build Up the Church of Jesus Christ (1 Cor. 14:12, 26)

The purpose of prophetic ministry isn't to honor men, but to equip and build up the Body of Christ through messages that *strengthen, build, edify, encourage, exhort, console, and comfort* her. These words represent a cross-section of the various translations of 1 Corinthians 14:3 that highlights this command. The singular direction from Paul regarding any prophetic message is the same: Love the Church.

He interrupted his own exposition on the gifts in 1 Corinthians 12 and 14 with a passionate plea to love the Church and one another, above all else, in 1 Corinthians 13. Without love, prophecy is a clanging cymbal and nothingness (1 Cor. 13:1-2).

A dear friend once challenged me that the prophetic gift will not be perfected in us until His love for the Church is perfected in us. Any accuracy in predictions, discernment of spirits, consistent words of knowledge, or anointing to impart wisdom is entirely pointless without His love infusing every spoken syllable. It is nothing. It's a mirage of ministry propped up by presumption and pride.

Just as in preaching, if we aspire to any hope of legitimacy in prophetic ministry, we must root out any treasonous, self-promoting motive, throw it on the altar of His mercy, and cry out to the Holy Spirit for a fresh revelation of His love for the Church.

This common yearning for authenticity in our love for the Church would be further validated in extending the right hand of fellowship toward each other.

We must endeavor pastorally and prophetically to strengthen, build, edify, encourage, exhort, console, and comfort each other as different, but equally important, members of the Body of Christ. There are certainly false teachers and prophets everywhere in the Church to discourage such an effort, but the failure of others' integrity should not excuse our own in any way.

Genuine preaching and prophetic ministry is demonstrated as Jesus said in John 13:35, "By this all people will know that you are my disciples, if you have love for one another."

In true preaching and prophetic ministry, we are first heralds of the holy love of God to His Church in our generation. I'm confident that a growing unity between the pastoral and prophetic ministry within the Church will have the same effect Paul intended for all the gifts, especially prophecy— encouragement, edification, and comfort.

2) A Sign of God's Manifest Presence (1 Cor. 14:25)

There is one more distinction of true prophecy and its purpose setting it apart from all other gifts and ministries that the apostle Paul highlights for us in 1 Cor.14:22b-25:

> ...prophecy is a sign not for unbelievers but for believers. If, therefore, the whole church comes together and all speak in tongues, and outsiders or unbelievers enter, will they not say that you are out of your minds? But if all prophesy, and an unbeliever or outsider enters, he is convicted by all, he is called to account by all, the secrets of his heart are disclosed, and so, falling on his face, he will worship God and declare that God is really among you.

True prophecy manifested in the church is intended to be a sign for *believers* (:22b) and *unbelievers* (:23) that God is *really* among us. The purpose of people gathering in a building each week to sing and listen to preaching about letters written thousands of years ago, is a stretch for most people. Common to unbelievers, I'm sure there are times when believers waver on the purpose of this weekly routine as well; especially when they don't feel close to God.

The worship and preaching can certainly be anointed and helpful to restore our sense of God's presence, but Paul says that when true prophecy comes forth it will produce a visceral reaction that causes people to hit the floor exclaiming, "God is REALLY among you!"

When anointed prophecy comes by the Spirit, there is an unmistakable sense that God Himself is there and using an imperfect person to speak to His people.

This may not be something you've experienced before, or maybe you've observed men who've turned prophecy into a self-serving sideshow, but Paul states that true prophecy is a sign of God's immediate and manifested presence among His people.

Believers receive the sign of encouragement, edification, and comfort because they aren't surprised by His presence. They already believed He is there. However, for the doubter or unbeliever who isn't sure, or doesn't know at all, they will be unable to contain themselves and will proclaim what everyone else already knows when true prophecy comes, "God is REALLY among you!"

The difference in the response of the believer and unbeliever is expectation. We must always gather as believers expecting the presence of God to be active, and true prophecy is a stated, biblical manifestation of His presence.

This is the Father's heart for His Church. He wants true prophetic ministry operating in the local church as another confirmation that He is really among us. God is delighted to be among His people, and true prophecy is a sign to His Church of that unchanging truth.

Do you see why it's critical we have prophecy in the local

church as the days grow darker in the world? Not as something that seeks to entertain us like a psychic reading; not as something that competes with preaching for superiority in the service; not as something that we have to fear because the gift is poorly understood, received, and delivered; not as something that is man-centered; but as a *sign* of His presence among us that draws our attention and affection to Him.

Whether corporately or individually, I am more amazed than ever at how a single prophetic message offered in obedience to God, under the anointing of the Holy Spirit, at the appropriate time can strengthen the saddened soul, restore hope to the hopeless, and build faith in the faithless. The Church needs to know His manifest presence of love, faithfulness, and encouragement to endure through the gifts...especially prophecy.

DIRECTION - What are the different gifts?

Chapter 4

The Gifts Are Operating In the Church

Even if lifeless instruments are played, there is a distinct sound—something recognizable and applicable. Paul used the distinction argument to reflect on the various ways he ministered as a leader to the Church. These differences are clearly demonstrated in the ways the Holy Spirit manifests His grace gifts.

Offices: Men Given by Christ to the Church

Ephesians 4:11 speaks of gifts, or offices, given to men at Christ's ascension. It says He gave some as apostles, prophets, evangelists, pastors, and teachers. These are continuing offices or leadership roles, geared to equip and build up His Church to maturity prior to His return.

Each gift/calling continues in individuals raised up within their generation as an ongoing expression of Christ's faithful love for His Church. Each man takes up the mantle to fulfill the work of equipping and building up the Church until He dies, or Christ returns. Regardless of how men have changed the titles by denomination or doctrine, the Holy Spirit is still using these offices to grow and mature His church. Changing the label to suit our interpretation of Scripture doesn't change what He is doing, or how He is using those He has chosen.

These are ministry gifts put in people directly chosen by

Christ, with resident callings distinct from periodic manifestations of the Spiritual gifts. They are given to the Church by His will, and accountable to Christ to fulfill those callings.

Spiritual Gifts - Gifts Given by the Spirit to the Church

The Holy Spirit made sure prophetic ministry remained in the New Covenant (Acts 11:28, 13:1, 15:32, 21:10), even knowing that we would have the Bible. He made sure the prophet was included in the gifts that Jesus gave to the Church (Eph. 4:11). He also commanded that we eagerly desire the gift of prophecy above all others (1 Cor. 14:1).

We need to reexamine the Holy Spirit's intent in elevating this gift. If we can understand the New Testament purposes of prophecy revealed in Scripture, then we may find ourselves appreciating afresh the prophetic ministry.

These spiritual gifts are known as *charismata*, or "gifts of grace" and are given individually to each believer according to 1 Cor.12:7 ("To each is given..."), as the Spirit wills. We each have gifts "that differ according to the grace given to us" (Rom. 12:6). The goal of all the spiritual gifts should be to "strive to excel in the building up of the church" (1 Cor. 14:12).

Each believer should know what grace gifts are flowing in them and earnestly desire the higher gifts, especially prophecy (1 Cor. 12:31, 14:1). The spiritual gifts are listed in different locations in Scripture. Below are listed the most notable spiritual gift locations. There are additional gifts noted in the Scripture such as celibacy, martyrdom, hospitality, missionary, and voluntary poverty, but for our purposes here, these are the most commonly discussed, and observed, "grace" gifts. Italicized gifts are mentioned in multiple verses:

> Romans 12
> exhortation
> giving
> leadership
> mercy

prophecy
service
teaching

1 Corinthians 12
administration
apostle
prophet
discernment
faith
healing
helps
knowledge
miracles
prophecy
teaching
tongues
tongues interpretation
wisdom

Ephesians 4
apostle
evangelist
pastor
prophet
teacher

It's interesting to note that the word *prophet*, or *prophecy*, occurs in all three lists of gifts. This isn't to highlight the importance of the person being used in prophecy, but rather the significance of the gift itself in Paul's mind to the Church. To recap, Paul elevates prophecy in 1 Corinthians 14, because it builds up the Church (:12) and it's a sign that "God is really among us" (:25).

Prophecy has been defined as speaking, or reporting, what God brings to mind. God speaks, we listen, and we share. That sharing can be in many ways and contexts, but if we shared something we believe God put on our heart for someone or a group, there's a good chance we prophesied.

We can change the term to "impression," or "thought," but the truth remains that if we attribute any of the revelation we received to the Holy Spirit, we prophesied. Demystifying this process puts prophetic ministry back within reach of the Church, right where it belongs.

But we can go too far. If we say it's just a counseling concept, or an insight of grace, we downplay the gift from God and the glory it affords Him. We have a chance in prophecy to draw everyone's attention and affection upward to God, but we can instead direct it toward men and their wisdom in sharing.

Does God need us to say it's a prophecy for anointing to flow? Absolutely not, but it's not a stretch to suggest that when we open our hearts to the flow of the Spirit in a ministry moment, we usually see the glory of God revealed in a unique way.

I was refused a job in an evangelical context because of my charismatic doctrinal position. In the exit meeting, this evangelical brother graciously shared that our doctrinal differences were a deal-breaker. But in his very next breath, he said he was praying for me before our meeting. He felt the Lord "impressed" something upon His heart about me.

This kind brother, who withheld a job because I believed in gifts and prophecy while he did not, was now going to share a prophecy he received about me in prayer before I arrived. He felt God showed him that I "would be given another opportunity very soon to be involved in Christian education" and that I "would be used mightily in the athletic arena."

He added that he sensed from the Lord that I might be prone to discouragement and that I wasn't to be upset by this setback, but that it was not the Lord's timing for this job.

He was right; a job as a Christian school Athletic Director soon followed.

In this brother's experience and doctrine, he had received an "impression from the Lord." The Bible calls that "prophecy." Was God any less glorified in how he shared?

No, but a wall of doctrinal distinction was raised that

diminished the glory rightly due God.

This brother received a clear prophetic message for me while disbelieving in prophecy. It was still a powerful and poignant life-changing prophecy for me, but what if this brother had a fully surrendered, faith-filled heart for God to speak to and through him? He has the door cracked open to hear to some degree, but what if he threw it open to the Holy Spirit?

This is the invitation of the prophetic for all of us, to experience the voice of God in a way that reveals Him in a greater form that doesn't leave any of us the same again.

If we hope to see God transform our lives and churches as we've prayed, we must be willing to move the dial of our doctrinal posturing from "impressions" from the Spirit to "immersion" in the Spirit as our only hope.

Chapter 5

Distinctions of Prophecy

1) The Prophecy of Scripture (2 Peter 1:20; 2 Tim. 3:16)

A guiding gift from the Spirit

The closed canon of Scripture is the central thrust of the Holy Spirit's fulfillment of His job description noted in John 14:26b: "...he will teach you all things and bring to your remembrance all that I have said to you." Peter references the Bible as "prophecy" (2 Peter 1:20) because that is what it is, uniquely inspired writings of men who were led by the Holy Spirit in a manner unique in all of human history. This Spirit-inspired compilation is the pinnacle of prophecy to men from God. There is nothing equal to it, nor will it be repeated or added to in any way, ever. However, this does not preclude the Holy Spirit from applying it, interpreting it, and working through it to reveal His present will to believers.

The Scripture contains His will and purpose for our lives, but it doesn't contain Him. It reveals Him in a measure He intends to all men, but His deeper revelation of Himself continues in each man's heart and in every genuine church through preaching *and* the gifts. The experience of the Spirit doesn't draw our attention away from Scripture; it highlights its value. It builds a desire to experience more of Him through the truths contained therein.

One clear normative revelation in Holy Scripture is followed by countless Spirit-led revelations of His attributes and ways when we apply Scripture. These lesser revelations guide us to a deeper understanding of who He is in His Word, who He is in our lives, and who He desires to be through us.

A great example of this Scripture/prophecy relationship I once heard was by Bojidar Marinov, a missionary to Bulgaria (www.bulgarianreformation.com). He likened the Scriptures to science as the fixed nature of things and prophecy to the discipline of engineering as the application of that science. Engineering doesn't do away with science; it draws from its foundation to meet specific applications and needs.

Ongoing prophecy applies scriptural truth and promises to our specific lives and situations; it doesn't add to Scripture or take away from it. It is a means of grace God gives to enrich our understanding of who He has revealed Himself to be in Scripture.

2) The Spirit of Prophecy (1 Sam. 10:10; 1 Cor. 14:31; Acts 19:6)

A presiding gift from the Spirit

As the One who is sanctifying the Church, the Holy Spirit presides over our meeting together as believers. He manifests Himself through the various means of grace gifts He appointed in Scripture (1 Cor. 12, 14; Rom. 12), which includes the ability of anyone indwelt by the Holy Spirit to prophesy as He gives the grace and faith to speak (1 Cor. 14:31). This presiding gift manifested through a person of His choosing by the sovereign Holy Spirit is an expression of His love, encouragement, edification, and comfort to the people of God. It also has those same benefits on the person being used. They stepped out in faith to share something they spontaneously received from the Holy Spirit and were blessed by His affirmation and confirmation of what they shared.

Does this mean God cannot speak outside the church building or use other sources than those specifically in the church to speak? No, it doesn't. He is sovereign over all and therefore can loose the tongue of a donkey to express His will (Num.

22:28) if He desires. He also spoke spontaneously through Saul in the Old Testament as a fulfillment of Samuel's prophecy over him (1 Sam. 19:24).

If the Holy Spirit desires, He can speak prophetically through anyone He chooses at any time, in any place. This is true of prophetic ministry within the church, as well as in evangelism. I recall receiving a word of knowledge and prophecy for a waitress while once sitting in a restaurant with friends. The Holy Spirit accurately revealed she had a boyfriend who did not know Christ and that she herself was being drawn back to Him. To affirm His love for her He told me to tell her that her boyfriend would be saved. She went away tearfully encouraged by the Spirit's ministry to her, where she was, in her workplace. I was so excited to be used by God like that, but He wasn't done that night.

Later, I left the restaurant so emboldened by the confirmation of the Spirit's work in that girl that I obeyed His prompting to share the gospel with another young man wandering in the parking lot. I simply said, "Hey, do you know Jesus?" He said, "No." I replied, "Would you like to? He loves you and died for your sins and He sent me over here to share some good news with you." That was all that was said and I expected to be rebuffed quickly. He said, "Yes, I would." No speeches or flowery words, just the truth as I understood it, and the Spirit moved on his heart. Amazingly, that young man enthusiastically accepted Christ right there on the spot!

As I rejoiced at God's faithfulness and told the story to my friends a few cars away, the young waitress I had prophesied over earlier stepped out of the restaurant and crossed the parking lot to the young man that had just received Christ and kissed him—it was the boyfriend God had promised to save! When I saw the kiss and recognized what the Spirit had done in fulfilling that prophecy that same night, I screamed aloud in the parking lot. My friends thought I'd lost my mind, but mine was a heart deeply affected by the privilege of seeing my simple obedience rewarded with a glimpse of the unsearchable riches of God's kindness through this gift!

Paul states that "all may prophesy one by one," (1 Cor. 14:31) and what the basic requirements are for this to occur in a gathering of the believers. This would be a "spirit of prophecy" operating within the church, or anywhere for that matter. Here, a speaker is used in the biblically labeled gift of prophecy, but it's not something they experience very often. This lack of frequency of use can be used to distinguish between those who operate in the gift of prophecy from time to time (spirit of prophecy) and those who seem to possess the frequency consistent with a resident gift (gift of prophecy).

When a "spirit of prophecy" comes on any person, in any place, at any time, it requires faith and obedience to speak, and all that is said must be tested by the truth of Holy Scripture and the witness of the Holy Spirit.

3) The Gift of Prophecy (Rom. 12:6; 1 Cor. 12:10; 1 Cor. 14:3)

An abiding gift from the Spirit

While anyone can prophesy, some are more active in sharing what the Holy Spirit is revealing to them. The genuine gift of prophecy in someone will typically be accompanied by an evident Christ-like character, humility, and faith. A person who operates in the gift of prophecy will usually receive impressions in multiple ways—dreams, visions, words of wisdom, words of knowledge, and various types of prophecy. Those who function in this gift are told to do so according to their proportion of faith (Rom. 12:6).

Paul is encouraging those who hear God this way not to strive in their efforts, but to function at the level of their faith. This could mean we have faith to share with just one person in one setting all the way up to corporate words for thousands. At either end of the spectrum, it is still faith governing the execution. Nothing changes in terms of the need to test what is said from the person used this way, but if the gift is genuine it will have all the marks of the true gift—accuracy, anointing, encouragement, exhortation, and comfort. (Chapter 21 addresses the testing of prophecy in depth.)

4) The Office of Prophet (Eph. 4:11; Acts 11:27-28, 13:1, 15:32)

A residing gift from Jesus

According to Ephesians 4:11, there are individuals given by Jesus Christ himself to fulfill the calling of prophet to the church. These persons are gifts to the Church from Jesus Christ. This can be a congregational prophetic call to a local church, and in some cases an extra-local call to serve the broader Church around the world. The scope of the prophet's gift will be discerned by those around him, and the Holy Spirit will make clear what He wants.

This confirmation will typically be recognized by the local pastoral leadership team, other prophets, apostles, and/or church leaders. This acknowledgment is usually made public through a commissioning and validation of their Ephesians 4 gift, a solemn charge to fulfill their ministry in obedience to the Spirit, and an increased responsibility and accountability of the prophet and leadership team caring for them.

He did it with Paul and Barnabas in Acts 13 by prophecy, and Timothy in 1 Timothy 4:14 when He confirmed callings and directed the elders to release his gift. These are men who not only prophesy, but also possess other gifts that qualify them to be used in leadership, teaching, and development of others.

They are called to equip the saints for works of ministry and build up the Church. The anointing on this person will be evident to all who are ministered to by them, and as their character grows, they will be released by the Holy Spirit to take their place alongside the elders in the church to care and provide for her.

These are not first-century Scripture-writing prophets, nor are they Old Testament prophets. They are generational, continuing prophets called to carry the mantle of God's grace for the Church in their lifetime, leaving a legacy for those they train and release for the next generation. They are not solo shows of prophetic ministry; they are servants who lead teams of prophetic voices in the Church as evidence of their call to equip and build up the Body.

Why the Distinctions of the Gift of Prophecy?

When leaders begin to distinguish between the spirit of prophecy, gift of prophecy, and office of prophet in someone, this would usually relate to the "sphere of influence" (measure of impact) that is discernible when they are used. It's not a measure of maturity or godly character; it's an awareness of how God appears to anoint the ministry of one person over another.

This fact that God sees difference in anointing and influence in His servants was clearly explained in Numbers 12:1-8, when Miriam and Aaron challenged Moses' anointing as a prophet. God clearly distinguished the anointing on Moses as a prophet as different from Miriam and Aaron in such strong terms that He severely punished them for their insubordination.

The differences of prophetic anointing on people being highlighted matter little to anyone not involved in prophetic ministry development. But when leaders are discerning God's grace on people for ministry, it can be helpful to have a simple template to measure.

The New Testament calls anyone who prophesied with some regularity a prophet (Agabus, Judas, Silas). Even in 1 Corinthians 14, prophetic people were noted as "prophets" ("... the spirits of prophets are subject to prophets", v. 32). Paul's use of *prophet* could have been a general reference to those who are being used prophetically. Instead of saying, "person used in prophecy" it would be easier to just say "prophet" to denote someone speaking from the Holy Spirit.

Therefore, we must be careful to communicate that these distinctions in the gift sphere are not about classifying the talent, performance, or significance of anyone. They are to help us clarify the nature, scope, and level of the grace gift being demonstrated in a person. This allows leaders to better track the development, maturity, and equipping of the believer, which is their scriptural mandate.

We are all in danger of selfish ambition and pride, but the greater danger to all prophetic people is *unbelief*. When a grace gift is identified in someone, there is a greater sense of responsibility and faith for that gift to grow in them. When they realize there may be a more frequent use in the gift of prophecy, there is an increased sensitivity and readiness to respond.

The labeling shouldn't be used to separate or exclude, but rather to build faith in those being used. Leaders can encourage people more specifically, "Hey John, every time there is that spirit of prophecy present during worship, I see you so willing to serve. Thank you for your obedience to the Spirit's prompting. Great word this morning." Or, "Hey Lisa, I really appreciate the growth I'm seeing in how God is using you in prophecy toward other women. The Holy Spirit has placed a rich gift in you; keep seeking the Lord for more."

In neither case was the focus on the label, but rather the faithfulness of God and their subsequent obedience. However, in a subtle way, the label speaks to the context and sphere of influence they are operating in. That is a wonderfully confirming, faith building, and validating encouragement to the prophetic heart.

Prophetic Ministry Authority is for Serving, not Subjecting

There is one more important distinction to be made in understanding the proper perspective on the gifts. No office, gifting, or position in the church is binding on anyone who does not choose to submit to it. A prophet may be recognized in one church, but that is not binding on anyone else to see him that way. The determination of someone as a "prophet" isn't authoritative in the sense that he can now dictate what others are to do. He is only being recognized for what God's grace provides through him in service to the Church.

None of the offices are designed to be dictatorial. They have authority as imputed by Christ as servants to the Church, and that is the extent of their calling. They have responsibility and limited authority related to what Jesus has apportioned to each for their ministry to operate effectively, but each believer is ultimately responsible to and under the authority of Jesus Christ.

A prophet cannot tell someone what to do, but only share what they believe God is saying in the moment. It's up to the believer to decide if that agrees with what they are sensing in their own hearts to do. If we choose to submit to the authority of the office out of obedience to the Holy Spirit who is guiding us, that is up to us.

The choice to submit to God-appointed earthly authority in the church is completely on the believer. The Holy Spirit will guide us to join a church, submit to the appointed authority there, and serve as He leads us for the purpose of demonstrating the grace of the gospel and rule of Jesus Christ upon our hearts. We are bound to Jesus, not men.

So any prophetic gift, or word, is never binding on anyone, unless the person chooses to accept what it says, in faith, to apply what God has revealed. No prophet has any control over anyone for any reason. They are the messengers of Jesus only and are not to think they can manipulate or lord anything over anyone in the use of their gift. Any effort of the prophet to exercise undue authority should be avoided. They are called to be servants, not to make others subservient.

Leadership considerations for evaluating where someone stands in their sphere* of prophetic ministry:

Spirit of Prophecy

Personal Fruit we believe God will develop
- Christians with a measure of faith to be used

Ministry Fruit we believe God will bring forth
- Builds up the Church with the following (1 Cor. 14:26):
  - Encouragement from God speaking extemporaneously

- Comfort from God with a picture, interpretation, application
- Exhortation from Scripture, poetry, wisdom, or spiritual song
- Word of knowledge, word of wisdom, and an exhortation
- Tongue and/or interpretation of tongue
- Communicates gift in a clear and compassionate manner
- Draws attention to God, His glory, and His purpose

Spirit of Prophecy Sphere of Ministry
- They are used *periodically* in the prophetic during meetings.

Gift of Prophecy/Prophet

Personal Fruit we believe God will develop
- Proven character, Christian, and member of the local church
- Pattern of growing maturity in Christ in life and family
- Faithful in the broader mission of the Church, not just gift
- Demonstrates a growing love for God's Church
- Garners respect of others without significant reservations
- Doctrinally sound on the gospel and the ongoing empowerment (infilling/baptism) of the Holy Spirit
- Observable humility and submission to authority
- Eager to receive constructive feedback

Ministry Fruit we believe God will bring forth
- Same as listed in Spirit of Prophecy

Additional Ministry Fruit of a Gift of Prophecy/Prophet
- Faith, accuracy, and depth consistent with a significant gift

- Ministers accurately in local/extra-local Church context
- Ministry consistently evidences the fruit of the Spirit
- Willing to work in team ministry as administrated by others
- Mature in handling predictive, corrective, or directive words

Gift of Prophecy Sphere of Ministry

- Discernible/distinguishable anointing for the gift
- Accurate at personal, corporate, leadership, extra-local level
- Is used *regularly* in prophecy and other gifts of the Spirit
- Consistent capacity to operate gift *submitted to authority*

Prophet Sphere of Ministry (beyond gift of prophecy)

- Discernible/distinguishable anointing for the *office gift*
- Accurate at personal, corporate, leadership, extra-local level
- Is used *significantly* in prophecy and *many* gifts of the Spirit
- Consistent capacity to operate in gift as *one with authority*
- *Imparting/Activating* anointing that stirs others to step out
- Proven ability to judge/administrate team prophetic ministry
- *Capacity to teach* the Word, train, equip, and raise up others
- *Possesses gifts of leadership and administration* seen by all
  (*Scope of ministry influence*)

In summary, here's what I believe is true from Scripture about prophetic ministry and its function in the Church.

1)   *We are called to be a prophetic people.* We preach a prophetic gospel message stating that Christ has come and will come again to set up His kingdom. This is "the prophetic word more fully confirmed" (2 Peter 1:19-21).

2)   *We are all able to prophesy.* That is to speak an utterance or thoughts spontaneously brought to mind, infused with the Spirit of God's anointing and influence on another person, or group of people (1 Cor. 14:31).

3)   *Prophecy is not equal to Scripture in authority on any level.* Scripture is the authority against which prophecy is measured (1 Thess. 5:19-21).

4)   *Prophecy is not to be despised, but rather tested against Scripture to ensure its veracity.* The revelation is pure, the person interpreting, applying, and sharing the word is not. The provision of testing is to protect the Church from the insertion of the flesh, selfish ambition, or sinful attitudes from the messenger. As in evaluating the preacher we are compelled to search out Scripture as good Bereans to assure that we are hearing the truth of God, in the same way we need to filter all we hear in the name of prophecy through Scripture to allow the Holy Spirit to maximize the blessing upon us (1 Thess. 5:21).

5)   *Prophecy builds up the Church through encouragement, exhortation, or comfort.* It is not a teaching, nor is it an expository rant on the sins of the people; it's a Spirit-led communication from God, pointing us to God, to receive from God (1 Cor. 14:3).

6)   *Prophecy must be done decently and in order.* The message should be "weighed" by other prophets and leadership of

the Church and each can speak when it's their turn. The spirit of the prophet is subject to the prophet. This means the word can be shared when its time under the control of the person being used (1 Cor. 14:40).

7)   *Prophecy is a gift "in part."* This means we see through a glass darkly and never have the full picture in any word we are given. The Holy Spirit does this to keep the focus on Him, and not the messenger (1 Cor. 13:9).

8)   *Prophecy is subject to the believer's will and obedience to Christ.* No prophecy in and of itself can do anything. It can only point to the work being done by the Holy Spirit. It's only the Holy Spirit that can apply any message or ministry to the heart of a person. No one should respond to a prophetic message without the express direction of the Holy Spirit in every moment. While most words are spoken in a manner that confirms and affirms a work the Spirit is already doing, there will be words that include future realities that belong completely to the sovereignty of God and should not be acted upon unless the Spirit is leading. And even then, it would be wise to include trusted leadership pastorally and friends who know us and our lives to assist in confirming the work of the Holy Spirit (Acts 13:1-3; 1 Thess. 5:19-21).

9)   *Prophecy is only possible by the Spirit through the gospel.* "For it is the spirit of prophecy who bears testimony to Jesus" (Rev. 19:10 NIV) and that testimony is the gospel of Jesus Christ's substitutionary sacrifice on the cross for sin and His subsequent resurrection from the dead. This good news is the foundation of all New Testament prophecy, and it should be saturated with it when it is shared.

Part 2: The Models of Prophecy

Introduction to Part 2

DISCERNMENT - *Where is the pastor's and church's current level of faith for the gifts and manifestations of the Spirit?*

This is the leadership's responsibility to discern where the congregation's hearts are situated with reference to the person and work of the Holy Spirit, especially the gifts, within their church. This includes assessing the church's corporate "eagerness" for prophecy. In this process, it's important that leaders have a clear vision of not only where they see the church now in relation to prophetic experience, but also where they wish to lead the church.

This requires us to consider what approach, or models, to consider in the development of this gift of prophecy.

Chapter 6

Prophetic Team Ministry:
A Better Way

There is ample evidence in Scripture (1 Sam. 19:20; Acts 11:26-27; Acts 13:1-3; Acts 15:32; 1 Tim. 4:14) of plurality in prophetic ministry. While individual prophetic voices are highlighted in both the Old and New Testament, there is usually a supporting cast of other unnamed prophetic people referenced. 1 Samuel 19:20 describes Samuel standing as "head over" the prophets who were prophesying in Naioth. This visual depiction of the teacher before his students, often referred to as "the school of the prophets," has become another key scriptural foundation for their grouping together in prophetic ministry.

There is another set of reasons for prophets often being found together. Prophetic people have a peculiar perception among many believers. Historically, they have been severely misunderstood, abused, and even killed for their ministry. While stoning the prophet is not an appropriate response under the New Covenant (1 Thess. 5:19-21), many prophetic people can still feel the effects of being severely ostracized or repositioned because of their ministry. Also, prophetic people can experience deep personal conviction, difficult life challenges, and disproportionate adversity as the Holy Spirit faithfully develops their humility and character. These all-too-common occurrences also contribute to prophetic persons seeking out one another, thus fulfilling the old idiom "birds of a feather flock together."

This concentration of prophetic persons coming together served, and still serves, many purposes, such as provision, support, training, accountability, and discipleship. Using modern vernacular, the "company of prophets" in today's church might better be termed a "team."

"Team" is a concept clearly understood and appreciated most for its higher purpose than any one individual. Also, teams by nature have a continual need for leadership to manage them, for discipleship to sustain them and for contexts to grow them. Prophetic team leadership comes from the Ephesians 4 gifts of the pastor and prophet called to equip and encourage the team. A prophetic team's discipleship springs from the relationships born of the Holy Spirit in doing life together. The prophetic team's context is the church, whose elders and members have Holy Spirit-given faith for a prophetic team to grow in grace to serve and edify the Body of Christ.

Modeling prophetic "team" ministry is intended neither to isolate, nor highlight, any unique significance in the church. Rather, like any other ministry in the church that needs to be grown from infancy, the team approach provides a protected, accountable, and safe environment for the Holy Spirit to encourage, edify, and mature believers into their biblical calling. As the church provides a similar protective, accountable, and safe covering for growth of all its members on a macroscopic level, this ministry team model—especially prophetic team ministry—serves as an incubating tool on the microscopic level for leadership teams to fulfill their Ephesians 4 call to encourage, equip, and mature the saints.

New Testament Scripture provides very limited teaching and descriptions of the Spirit's prophetic activity in the church. However, there is enough we can glean from these ministry moments to sketch out a working understanding of some of the roles played by New Testament prophecy in the early Church. I believe this severely limited teaching and narrative of the Holy Spirit's use of the prophetic was His way of ensuring the Church's continued focus on the gospel going forth, while maintaining the appropriate dependence upon Him at every level for the gift's manifestation.

Leadership teams and prophetic people have enough Scriptural evidence to see its place and function in the New Testament church as *congregational prophetic ministry* (Agabus stood among the believers—Acts 11:27-30), as *leadership-serving prophetic ministry* (prophets and teachers together seeking God for His will for the Church—Acts 13:1-3), as *"team" prophetic ministry* to encourage the believers (Judas and Silas encouraged the brothers—Acts 15:32), as *personal prophetic ministry* to individuals (Agabus prophesied over Paul—Acts 21:11), and as *presbytery prophetic ministry* (elders and prophets together ministered to and laid hands on Barnabas and Saul—Acts 13:1-4; Paul and the elders laid hands on Timothy and imparted a gift—1 Tim 4:14).

These various ministry moments have been stitched together into the infographic model below to better visually capture what we're seeking for the Holy Spirit to do prophetically for our churches.

This model provides us some administrative direction to consider for the gift's various functions in the Church, a path to faith for prophetic ministry to the Church, and insight into the ways He uses various people to grow this ministry for the Church. The single objective of this model is to provide a series of biblically anchored guardrails for how prophecy can be a vibrant, scripturally stable, and God-honoring addition to the life of the Church today. With so much abuse, self-promotion, and ignorance about this gift rampant in churches, I hope to use this model as a means of grace to re-envision leadership teams through the simplicity of what Scripture says, combined with my years of experience serving in submitted, proven prophetic ministry to a local church and its leadership team.

A glossary is included at the back of this book to define unfamiliar terms, or my definitions of common ministry terms that may have different nuances from church to church. Also, this model is not intended to be an exhaustive visual depiction of prophetic ministry in Scripture. God's Word is replete with prophetic experiences that occur outside the gathering of the people of God in both the Old and New Testaments; I have intentionally restricted this infographic to New Testament references in the book of Acts to highlight only the most relevant content to our focus on pastors and the local church.

PROPHECY AND PROPHETIC TEAM MINISTRY IN THE LOCAL CHURCH

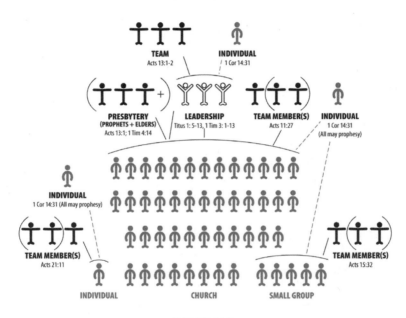

LEGEND

CHURCH - The gathered expression of the Body of Christ in the local community (Heb. 12:23; 1 Peter 2:9; Acts 2:42-47)

LEADERSHIP - Any governmental structure, or polity, that oversees the local expression of the Body of Christ (Titus 1:5-13; 2 Tim. 3:1-13; 1 Tim. 4:14)

ȶȶȶ

PROPHETIC TEAM - Any group of local church members recognized and recruited by local church leadership team to serve alongside, grow with, and be accountable to one another in the ministry of prophecy to the Body of Christ (Acts 15:32; Acts 11:27; Acts 13:1)

ȶ(ȶȶ)

TEAM MEMBER(S) - Any combination of individual or gathered prophetic team members present during a ministry moment (Acts 11:27; Acts 21:11; Acts 15:32)

INDIVIDUAL - Any believer filled with the Holy Spirit used in corporate vocal ministry to the congregation or is used in a ministry moment to a small group or individual (1 Cor. 14:31)

ȶȶȶ+ɣɣɣ

PRESBYTERY (PROPHETS & ELDERS) - Any team prophetic ministry where elders and/or prophets are ministering together over an individual, small group, or congregation; usually accompanied by the laying of hands (1 Tim. 4:14; Acts 13:1-3)

Modeling New Testament Prophetic Ministry, Not "New" Revelation

This model visually depicts the various ways the Holy Spirit manifested prophetic ministry in the New Testament to serve the Church. Although there are only a few Scriptures that highlight specific prophetic ministry, it's clear from the diversity of descriptions that the Spirit interwove this gift into the fabric of everyday life in the Church. The multiple ways it was demonstrated also confirms that the Holy Spirit intended for this gift to be broadly integrated and edifying to the local expression of the Body of Christ.

To suggest this powerful and edifying prophetic ministry has ceased today is to declare the Spirit has ceased encouraging and empowering believers for His glory in all these ways depicted.

The absence, abstinence, or abuse of personal prophetic experience is not grounds for disobedience to the Holy Spirit. It's not a suggestion or optional ministry based on denomination; we are all commanded to prophesy (1 Cor. 14:1, 31, 39; 1 Thess. 5:19-21). Nor does the belief in the closed canon of Scripture suddenly disqualify believers from being used by the Spirit to do the powerful works of ministry written in it (Eph. 2:8-9).

Scripture is our perfect prophetic message preached, prophesied, and promoted by His Spirit in multiple contexts of ministry. To redefine or reposition prophecy out of our churches to suit our understanding, interpretation, fear, or comfort level of the Holy Spirit's activity is to relegate His most edifying and needed ministry to the past.

Prophecy is feared to be a "new" revelation beyond the canon and thus is considered by some to be heresy. I would submit that interpreting and relegating the Holy Spirit's gifts, signs, and wonders to the past from the pulpit is tantamount to declaring there is a "new" revelation of an "enlightened" church having a form of godliness that denies its power (2 Tim. 3:5). The church of Scripture is a powerful one infused with the ministry of the Holy Spirit, and any attempt by leaders to placate those offended by what they do not know or understand by explaining it as "ceased" is substantially more heretical.

We will gladly accept that the Holy Spirit could speak to and through first-century believers in specific and powerful ways (through prophecy) for their encouragement, strengthening, and edification, but now that we have the Scripture complete, that same Holy Spirit has now effectively stopped doing what He Himself commanded us to keep doing in the same Scripture He wrote?

The entire logic process of cessationism is severely flawed and significantly more dangerous to the long-term health of the Church than any concern about prophetic inaccuracy and its impact on believers. This is not because prophecy is so special we can't do without it as a church; that has clearly proven not to be the case.

No, the great tragedy of cessationism is the subtle elevation of what man has to say about God in his own words, while assuming that because God wrote words down in Scripture that He is somehow finished talking about who He is in the midst of a Church He died for and desperately loves. Or worse, that His Holy Spirit wrote us a long set of notes (Bible) on how to live and then decided to sit back and see what we would do.

It is utter blasphemy to suggest the Bible is just a "set of notes" on how to live, and that the Holy Spirit left us a big love note and bolted; it is equally blasphemous to so venerate Scripture in our experience that we no longer treasure deeply the active manifest presence and power of the Holy Spirit spoken of in Scripture.

This model is not offered as an argument against cessationism, nor is it an invitation to legalism, structure, and rules. It's a celebratory sketch of the Holy Spirit's broad and faithful prophetic ministry to His church in Scripture. It's also an appeal to prayer for the same in our day.

We are prone to organize and administrate as those who desire to be in control, which is why I believe the Holy Spirit intentionally limited His explanation of prophetic ministry and its operation. This is His ministry to and through the Church for His glory alone, and while we are identifying the biblical scope of that prophetic ministry in the New Testament in this picture as a means of better understanding how He works, we are not seeking to make doctrine or dogma from it.

Each leadership team should only be convinced in their own mind. They should be filled with faith as led by the Holy Spirit to implement what they believe would honor God in their congregation. It's only my intention to challenge our current level of faith as leaders for the purpose of exhorting each to examine their own heart regarding their commitment to obey all the Holy Spirit has commanded in Scripture.

Another way to consider this would be to answer the question "If we agreed with the command of Scripture to prophesy in the church and there was no abuse or misuse because it was perfect, would we embrace its use for our congregation?"

If the answer is yes, then you are not a cessationist, you are an environmentalist. That is not to suggest any hyper-political or regulatory motive in the broader cultural sense. Simply defined, environmentalists are concerned with the treatment and protection of the environment.

In the same way, if we believe in the gifts, but struggle with the way their self-serving abuse negatively impacts the church's environment, we are concerned with the gift's improper administration, not with whether it exists. This is the contention of those who take the continuationist position mentioned earlier. We want the Giver (Holy Spirit) and we want the gifts, but we don't want the grossly caricatured and disfigured image of the Holy Spirit painted by those who profess His power. Many lack the maturity, character, and humility to demonstrate a truly God-glorifying ministry that manifests the power of the Holy Spirit without pretense or abject self-promotion.

The good news is that as God-ordained leaders in the church we are uniquely positioned and empowered to create a better environment that is protected and more productive for prophetic ministry to serve and thrive. We shouldn't fear prophecy as leaders; we should be faithfully administrating it in our churches for the glory of God.

This is where I hope to serve leaders with the rest of this book. Not seeking to defend something already clearly stated as a command in Scripture, but rather to map a scripturally sound process that cuts through the fog of fear and abuse and builds faith for a thriving prophetic future in His local church.

The first step in that process begins with a team.

Building After the True Model of Team

God Himself, the all-powerful "three-in-one," is the truest definition of Team Ministry that exists. The Father, Son, and Holy Spirit as three distinct persons in One, working to fulfill His will, is our clearest demonstration of team ministry. 1 Cor. 12:4 speaks directly of their team ministry function with the gifts, "Spirit...Lord [Jesus]...God [Father]." If team ministry is who He is, then we must align ourselves in like manner.

He is the only expert in all things "Team." There is no source of team building that can approach what God can do with the hearts of men for His glory. Look at what He did with a rag-tag group of fishermen and social outcasts; He changed them, brought them together, and it was said of them, "These men who have turned the world upside down have come here also" (Acts 17:6).

God can bring together ministry teams by His power that will shake their world for Him. We, as leaders, must be willing to ask Him to give us men and women who share our passion for His gospel, His glory, and His grace gifts. We need Him to knit our hearts together for His purpose. His nature is team ministry, and He will form His nature in us as a testimony of His glory to an individualistic, self-serving, self-promoting world.

Chapter 7

Pastors Model Team Ministry

The strongest model for a prophetic team is that of your local leadership team (pastors, administrators, deacons, elders, directors, or whatever your church calls its team of leaders). The elder team is the pastors' richest legacy and gift to other team ministries seeking to grow within the local church. How they love one another is what Jesus said would set them apart and signify their being true disciples of Christ. The elder team in the local church, regardless of gifts and talents combined, will only be as effective as their willingness to love one another.

Blessed with a strong elder team, the prophetic team I lead was based on what we saw lived out in our church day after day and week after week. Our elder team was started by a man whose passion for the Church, the gospel, and New Testament reality is unmatched, in my experience. His example of faithful team leadership has been an inspiring example.

The measure of this elder team's effective leadership was, and still is, their humility, integrity, perseverance, and faith. How our pastors demonstrated love for one another through genuine relationship, conflict resolution, project completion, and ministry deference has been a powerful and effective means of grace. We recognized it as the ideal example for the development of our prophetic ministry team in the local church.

There is no perfect church, only a perfect Savior. As a prophetic person in a local church, I've seen volumes of good, some bad, and even truly dark seasons, but there has been one unmistakable priority our leaders sought to preserve in their relationships wherever possible—their partnership in the gospel (Phil. 1:5).

Through disagreements, departures, disappointments, and church discipline, I've seen a continual effort toward restoration, reconciliation, and renewal coming out of every failure. There's been a pattern of elevating the purpose of Christ above pettiness, presumption, and pride.

Pastors should examine their commitment to exemplifying Christ-honoring team ministry as the basis for reproducing other ministry teams around them.

Pastors must humbly self-assess and apply the necessary steps for growth for themselves and their primary elder teams, for anything they hope the Spirit will do through them in others will correlate directly to their own leadership example.

Prophetic Team Ministry Is an Effective Model

While individual prophets were highlighted in the Old Testament for the significance of their contribution, there is substantial evidence for prophets ministering together in groups. Each prophetic ministry moment noted in the New Testament had multiple prophets present, despite a singular voice being recorded (Acts 11:27, Acts 13:1, Acts 15:32, Acts 21:9-10). We aren't made fully aware of the nature of these relationships, but it's safe to assume there was some relationship between them.

Our local church prophetic team has visited many churches, and in one visit we were told, "We are so grateful for your visit. You have shown us what New Testament prophecy in a team setting looks like, and now we can do it, too!" That is a big part of our call to New Testament prophetic ministry: equipping others by example and with hope for how God can use them to serve their local church together.

Paul referenced that gifts were imparted through the laying on of hands and prophecy in Timothy's life by the council of elders (presbytery), a team (1 Tim. 4:14). This team-oriented impartation changed Timothy's life, and God continues to do so with prophetic ministry teams that seek to honor Him.

Prophetic ministry in a team format can mean as few as two members working together. How teams are split up for ministry is up to the elders of the church, but the teaming concept is about strengthening the prophetic ministry by coming together to serve (Eccl. 4:12).

Leadership certainly has the authority to divide the team to minister to more people at once, but it is often best to have experienced team members join with less experienced members to teach and assist.

Prophetic team ministry builds up the prophets as they seek to build up the Church, and it provides them a number of unique blessings that aren't present when a single person is ministering alone.

1)   *Team ministry allows more "parts" to be shared or fit together in a time of ministry.*

Since they prophesy "in part" (1 Cor. 13:9), this means one person doesn't always get the whole picture of the Holy Spirit's ministry to someone. Team ministry provides a more complete ministry picture, to encourage and strengthen the church members. It also removes the pressure from any one person to do all the ministry. The Holy Spirit often strings together multiple parts to reveal His sovereign control and care for the recipient.

2)   *Team ministry allows time for the prophetic team to hear God between sharing times.*

From a purely group dynamic perspective, a team approach allows deeper and wider coverage. A single person offering prophetic ministry alone to a group spends a lot of time sharing and not as much time listening. With a team of people engaged in the ministry, some members can share while the others listen to the Spirit, perhaps gaining clarification and further insights from the Holy Spirit.

3)   Team ministry protects the members from pride.

In true prophecy, the shared word is from the Holy Spirit, through the vessel of the prophet. In a group meeting, people often cannot remember which team member said what during a ministry time, allowing genuine transfer of glory to God. Speaking for God can be heady stuff, tempting frail human vessels to think more highly of themselves than they ought. Team ministry assists in diffusing the focus and intensity of that struggle.

God will not share His glory with men, and prophetic team ministry thwarts the enemy's effort to encourage theft of God's glory in the heart of man.

4)   Team ministry increases faith in the members for ministry.

Faith is the essential catalyst of prophetic ministry, and faith flows free when the team is together in serving the Church. This faith for the prophetic is not a general hope that God will answer prayers, nor is it a reckless, boisterous effort to work people into a frenzied state. It's a mutual awareness among the members, witnessed by the Holy Spirit in each of them, that the Father is desirous to express His great love for His Church through the prophetic.

The amount and accuracy of prophetic ministry is significantly increased when this assurance of the Father's love being poured out is present. The evidence of this great faith released in prophetic ministry is an increased specificity in things only known to individuals, a palpable tenderness in the content being delivered, and the joy that pours forth in all present.

5)   Team ministry provides additional protection against error.

If needed, the team can quietly confirm what they are hearing with one another before sharing publicly.

This is very helpful when words are very specific or might need adjustment. It requires humility and trust to run things by each other, but the result is a more focused and edifying message.

6)   *Team ministry demonstrates a model that the local church being ministered to can easily follow.*

Since there is no emphasis on a single gifted person, the church is not only built up, but is given a road map to future ministry within their own church, serving their own people.

If churches are still learning how to develop the prophetic ministry gifts, they can still serve very effectively in a group led by a pastor/elder. This is how our team started as we were learning, and the elder provided covering, accountability, and credibility to the prophetic ministry.

7)   *Team ministry provides accountability and feedback for each serving member, to grow and develop in their use of the gifts.*

The congregation may not see this critical component of the prophecy team, but it's vital to its members. Members can seek insight from others on the team. Ideally, each member enthusiastically pursues feedback, demonstrating humility, but as individuals who regularly provide insight to others, if accountability is required, it should be administered and received with grace.

8)   *Team ministry models unity for the local church's use of the spiritual gifts.*

Individuals are encouraged when they see an active prophetic team ministry modeling open interaction between the members during ministry.

This is a critical component for an elder team's consideration of bringing a team in. A visiting team's example of conversation regarding words and thoughts they receive done in front of the local church members demystifies the process and brings a measure of faith to duplicate what they see.

9) *Team ministry encourages pastoral care because it is set up to include the pastor's input during the ministry time.*

The team members waiting to minister can be conferring with the pastor throughout the ministry time, confirming specific words; assuring proper handling of sensitive words of prediction, direction, or correction; and securing confidence to impart various gifts as led by the Holy Spirit.

Misapplication, or misinterpretation, is a real danger without this type of interaction, and it provides the pastor with a faith-building mechanism for influence and administration.

Prophetic team ministry is not a psychic performance requiring secretive actions and dramatic buildup from team members. This is a very powerful, highly impacting ministry that operates best when approached with humility before God, sensitivity to God-ordained authority, and consideration of the leadership's responsibility for the local church.

10) *Team ministry provides a context for Ephesian 4 prophets to develop and mature.*

Team ministry provides all the necessary ingredients of relationship, accountability, and opportunity to see legitimate prophets rise to their God-ordained place in serving the local and extra-local Church. Over time, the intentional creation of a prophetic ministry team will bear the fruit of the Holy Spirit's development of Ephesians 4 prophets.

The future of the unified Church operating in the power of the Holy Spirit won't be focused on persons and their gifts, but rather the mission of the gospel going forth. The Holy Spirit is raising up a generation of New Testament prophetic voices that are committed to God's glory, His gospel, and the maturing of the Body of Christ through equipping team ministry.

We need to recognize that God is already communicating with his people, giving them prophetic words and images for the local church. How are they to share these insights if not during the gathering of the church? The Church of Corinth struggled with this, giving us an example of what not to do. There, believers stood where they were, interrupted and spoke over each other, and ran roughshod over the gathering. Paul didn't want to quell prophecy; he wanted to bring order and protocol to better present prophecy. Today, some still use open congregational sharing during pauses in worship, and others use a microphone at the front of the church, where individuals who want to share are allowed, at appointed times and with vetting from an elder, to speak to the gathering. In either case, in the early days of such a ministry, you can expect it to be raw and prone to over-sharing, but it's a learning process and a great feeder system for a prophetic team.

Who does God seem to use most frequently and with alignment to the Holy Spirit? You will probably find that these individuals make a practice of being silent before the Lord, truly listening. They aren't more "Christian" than anyone else; they probably just work at private meditation more than others.

These individuals are potential core team members. This team is built by God to promote His glory to serve the Church, so do not allow preference or prejudice to enter into your evaluation. Guard against the very real possibility that those who God uses prophetically in the service may not be whom the elders would pick for the team. Samuel found out when pursuing David to anoint him as King that God looks not on the outward appearance but on the heart (1 Sam. 16:7).

Chapter 8

Starting Prophetic
Team Ministry from Scratch

Prophetic team members aren't judged with elder-level requirements from Scripture. The first steps of building a prophetic team should be discipleship-focused, not prophecy-focused. Build relationships and a context to serve, not elevation in ministry. God often chooses unlikely vessels for His service. God isn't swayed by financial status, age, beauty, or race; He seeks individuals who will listen to Him.

Who Should Be Considered To be on a Local Church Prophetic Team?

When building a prophetic team ministry, two groups will take focus. There will be those who are used from time-to-time, who love the Church and enjoy being used periodically in the gift through ministry. And there are those who God uses more frequently, who love the Church and are pursuing all God wants to do through a growing gift ministry. Both groups should be regularly engaged to serve the local church in prophecy, but for the purposes of team ministry, the second group is your core team.

1)   *They are gospel-centered, Bible-preaching, Jesus-loving Christians*
        A critical element of New Testament prophetic

ministry is grace, which is best demonstrated and understood in the gospel of Jesus Christ. The Bible is the standard against which all prophecy is tested and therefore Bible knowledge must richly dwell in the believer (Col. 3:16). Their love for Jesus must be evident, as "the testimony of Jesus is the spirit of prophecy" (Rev. 19:10).

2)   *They are a man/woman of observable godly character*

Authenticity of spirit and life in Christ are the measures of a true prophetic person. Any falsehood found in the prophetic person is character-based first and foremost, not in the inaccuracy of words they share.

3)   *They have a significant, ongoing, infilling experience with the Holy Spirit (baptism)*

There is an evident, ongoing renewal (baptism) of the Spirit in their lives demonstrated in joy, boldness, gift manifestation, and the fruits of the Spirit. A growing relationship with the Holy Spirit is imperative for prophetic ministry to mature and serve.

4)   *They are committed members in the local church where they serve*

Ministry without membership is itinerant speaking. The first validation of the prophetic person is their commitment to love and serve the Church of Jesus Christ in the local expression where the Spirit leads them. In the absence of this commitment to a local church, there is little that suggests they value what the prophetic person must demonstrate in their ministry: humility, accountability, authority, and submission.

5)   *They are not a brand new, or immature, believer*

Immaturity is not a sin; however, it can lead to things that can hinder the Spirit's work in others. It's best to ask those needing growth to step back from any public team ministry until they have built maturity and knowledge. This does NOT mean young people aren't ready for a team. Maturity is never measured by chronological age but by character and depth.

6)   *They have a growing love for their local church (not bitter, gossiping, or slandering others)*

Members who have unresolved issues with other members or the leadership will not grow in faith on the team. They will tend to poison the team with harsh critique and uncharitable judgments. Love for the local church is where the true reality of the believer's faith and love is demonstrated. Love for the global Church is only genuine if there is love for their local brothers and sisters.

7)   *They have a practice of humility evident in their faith and relationships*

Humility is the first attribute in the development of the prophetic team; it precedes all the grace the Spirit will give in any context through this ministry (James 4:6). This will be a key aspect of their willingness to submit to team leadership, work within the team, and deliver ministry that bears lasting fruit.

8)   *They are sound in their understanding of the core doctrines of the faith*

Mountaintop experiences from prolonged exposure to the Spirit reveal the grace and love of God; regular seasons of wandering in the wilderness build humility and dependency on God. Both of these states are common to the prophetically gifted. A solid foundation in core doctrines of Scripture roots these individuals, preventing them from being tossed about by every wind of doctrine that draws their minds away from the truth of Scripture.

9) *They have faith to prophesy in front of people with boldness and clarity (not anxious in front of people)*

It takes self-control and capacity to speak in front of other people. This and the ability to flow prophetically in settings where they may be observed by a large number of people is a necessity for this team.

10) *There is Holy Spirit anointing and empowerment present when they prophesy*

The truest test of the prophetic person is the witness of the Spirit in the other members of the team and elders. When they prophesy, there should be an evidence of the Holy Spirit manifesting God's presence through them.

11) *The prophetic/leadership team bears witness of their gift and character*

Beyond the character the prophetic person demonstrates in their personal life, they also must show character in how they minister alongside other team members and before others in ministry. This must be validated by the pastors and team.

12) *They demonstrate a measure of accuracy as confirmed by those assessing and receiving*

A prophetic ministry without increasing accuracy is not prophetic; it's in danger of being presumptuous and must be addressed before being allowed to continue. Accuracy is not the only measure, but it's necessary for inclusion in more frequent ministry.

13) *The fruit of the Spirit is evident in their prophetic delivery and response to input and correction*

The prophetic person must demonstrate an increasing evidence of the fruit of the Spirit listed in Gal. 5:22, both in their delivery of the message and how they receive correction and feedback regarding their message.

14) *They are precise and concise in interpretation and application of their words*

This is a developed skill within the prophetic, but each member should be able to edit and apply what they hear from God without adding anything just to be heard or understood better.

15) *They are seeking and experiencing multiple manifestations of the gift (visions, dreams, words)*

They are capable of receiving prophetic ministry in many ways to serve the Church. They understand the Holy Spirit develops the gift in them by changing the way He speaks, building their faith and trust, not creating anxiety in them.

16) *They are not significantly prone to fear of man, failure, or lost approval*

Prophetic people who are prone to approval issues are better in smaller contexts until the Holy Spirit can develop them further. Members of a growing prophetic ministry team who struggle in these qualities may not become prophets, but certainly can assist in the development of others desiring to be used in the gift. Not everyone will have an equal anointing in the prophetic ministry, but team ministry is about each member helping others grow in whatever way they contribute. Some will be called to the level of Ephesians 4 ministry within the team, and when they are ready to be commissioned, they will become the leaders of the prophetic ministry team. The prophet should be a proven, mature, and grounded member whose calling is clear to all who know them.

What Is a New Testament Prophet/Prophetess?
Who Qualifies and Commissions Them?

A New Testament prophet/prophetess is a man or woman, called by Christ to fulfill the prophetic ministry to equip, build up, and mature the Body of Christ. They communicate what they believe God is saying to the Church and develop others to do the same. The sphere of the prophet's influence (local and extra-local), as is the depth and clarity of their gift, is determined solely by the Holy Spirit.

There are also individuals who prophesy freely as they minister, heeding a call to ministry but not specifically to prophetic ministry. They display the gift of prophecy but may be a teacher or pastor, not a dedicated prophet. The elder team is tasked with identifying and maturing the prophets without drawing the other group away from their called ministry. Eventually, the elders can commission prophets to fulfill their Ephesians 4 calling to serve, equip, and build up the Church.

Chapter 9

Things to Avoid in Team Ministry Development

Hierarchal Divisions

Avoid identifying individuals simply for the sake of title or rank within the group (Executive Prophet, Master Prophet, etc.) All are encouraged to submit to one another out of love for Christ (Eph. 5:21). If a person is commissioned as a prophet and leader of the team, it's only for the purpose of serving the prophetic team as an equipper and encourager of others' ministry. Their calling requires they be more concerned with the local church team's development than the growth of their own ministry opportunities.

A "Have and Have Not" Mentality

The goal is to build up and look for ways to encourage others in how God is working in and through them. All members should avoid exclusivity or inappropriate self-promotion. The goal is not to recruit people to join a team, but rather as team members to equip others through love and relationship, with the understanding and faith to be used by the Holy Spirit in the gift.

This means that existing team members are always inviting, discipling, encouraging, and seeking others to participate in the prophetic for the building up of the Church. Team members become equippers and builders of the Body the moment they are included. They should never see themselves as anything other than servants of the Body of Christ with the grace He provides.

Pressure To Perform

The gospel must be infused into everything, preventing people from the demand to perform prophetically. Sometimes God doesn't speak. The pressure to perform means a team member may invent an impression. Guard against this temptation by extending grace to every team member.

Ministry impact is totally dependent on the Holy Spirit and His work, and while each member bears responsibility for what they say, there should be no expectation higher than that their communication be "decently, and in order" (1 Cor. 14:40).

Fear of Being Evaluated

Each team member must be willing to seek input, be evaluated through questions, and respond humbly. For team members doing the evaluating, remember the goal is to develop faith for more ministry. Harsh correction feeds the fear of being evaluated and misses the goal of correction. To develop prophetic ministry, assessment must be dripping with faith and encouragement for those who stepped out publicly.

Sensitivity To Others' Empowerment

At times, the Holy Spirit will empower one person more than another, use one more often, or grant more specificity. There are a number of reasons God may give greater empowerment:

- The individual may be a prophet/prophetess being raised up
- The Holy Spirit desires to encourage/bless the one being used
- The minister's preparation for the meeting in fasting/ prayer
- The Spirit is establishing credibility of gift to the team/leadership

It's important that the other members not grow envious or jealous of the opportunities given to one another. Train your teams to rejoice in the growth of the gifts in everyone, as the Spirit wills, and resist the temptation to resent another's promotion.

Things Pastors Can Do That Will Develop Healthy Prophetic Ministry

Encourage your prophetic team ministry to be tested and grown

1) Meet with individual ministry team members regularly to understand and grow their gift.

2) Have regular teaching workshops for prophetic growth.

3) Encourage use of their gift in care (small) groups and encourage care group leader feedback.

4) Have post-service prayer times with small groups of 2-3 prophetic people administrated by an experienced prophetic person or an elder.

5) Record prophetic ministry for review and feedback in all contexts.

Create Contexts for Prophetic Team Ministry to be Used

A prophetic person needs to be able to practice prophecy. There are certainly times after Sunday service and in care group settings for one-on-one prophecy, but with no one to give feedback, who will be trained? They need someone more experienced to be with them in the use of the gift, or an elder-pastor, who can talk them through what they heard and shared.

There are suggestions throughout this book for providing prophetic ministry contexts. However, the corporate prophetic "pump" will need to be primed through intentional contexts created for this ministry to be used and trained simultaneously. Expecting it to just happen on its own in the flow of the church's growth is not going to be enough to see it mature properly. Using planned contexts for prophetic ministry to be shared and trained will accelerate learning and confidence in those being used.

Prophetic people will invite training and input and respond to intentional, structured development contexts for ministry. Step out in faith to generate contexts and provide a safer, elder-served, non-threatening environment to share the gift openly. Faith and confidence will grow through helpful, compassionate input.

Experienced prophetic people can drive these contexts for the pastor. This allows potential prophets to develop their gifts of leadership, prophetic administration, teaching, and mutual accountability. In my church experience, we began with a pastor over the prophetic ministry in regular ministry training meetings (contexts). Now we continue to grow with trusted, experienced prophetic men who lead these meetings with elders attending, as able. It's a wonderful way to build.

In the absence of these meaningful contexts, prophetic people may come to believe they are on their own and seek outside contexts to grow, independent of the elder team, such as with online ministries or other outside prophetic ministries. While no one should stop individuals from pursuing such training, such a person may believe that now that they are "trained" they are able to minister in the local church. The problem is, such a member is not in relationship with the pastors, contexts are not established, and a frustrated prophetic church member feels marginalized.

Over the years, I have benefited greatly from a number of outside resources. However, I have always related what I'd learned to fellow prophetic team members and the leadership team so we can all benefit and grow together in our understanding of this ministry.

If God is working among us—and He is—then leaders indifferent to prophetic development will find their prophetic people drifting away from the local church, which does not serve the biblical intent of the prophetic. In addition, a lack of prophetic ministry contexts in the local church can encourage frustrated prophetic individuals to create their own, unaccountable, personal ministry meetings, self-promoting home gatherings of believers. None of these initiatives on their own are wrong, but if the leader's motive for isolating prophetic ministry is frustration, resentment, or self-promotion, the prophetic person is in danger of drifting into serious error.

There is potential for great discord if problems surface from gossip, slander, and bitterness during these prophetic ministry meetings. Even the most well-intentioned ministry offering could slip into confusion, frustration, and disillusionment if these attitudes are permitted. This will only increase the collateral damage that the local pastors have to deal with afterward in counseling people harmed by unguided, unaccountable prophecy.

The other end of this spectrum is just as disillusioning; gifted prophetic people without contexts to serve will assume the ministry isn't important to leadership and won't stir up their gift to serve the church beyond a periodic word here and there. Taking their cues from the absence of input and faith from the elders, they draw the conclusion that it is of no value. No leadership team wants to quench the Spirit, but that is literally what happens if prophetic members are ignored or overlooked.

There is a sort of self-fulfilling "prophecy" that occurs when leaders don't really believe in prophecy, avoid its inclusion, and declare it ceased. When any ministry does come forth that is immature and incomplete, they feel exonerated and justified in their original position and avoid the gift altogether. Tragically, what many aren't realizing is that it is their God-ordained responsibility to cultivate and equip the very lack of maturity they are accusing their members of. Instead of strengthening their members' understanding and growth in their gifts, they are using their weakness in the gift as their excuse to avoid the clear command of Scripture for individuals to prophesy and leaders to lead.

To avoid these two extremes, pastors must not ignore prophetic ministry development, nor should they allow the prophetic ministry to dictate what they do as a local church. Like any fruit-bearing tree, God the Holy Spirit will grow the seed of faith for prophetic ministry as long as it is planted in the soil of a thriving church, with the proper balance of warmth (care/relationships), light (contexts/meetings), water (Scripture/accountability), and fertilizer (feedback).

Chapter 10

Contexts for Prophetic Ministry

There are many kinds of contexts for prophetic ministry within the church. This list begins with a general context for those interested in growing in the gift, no matter what level they have, and funnels down to increasing levels of accountability for those with more experienced gift ministries.

This list is not exclusive or exhaustive, but each context is a means of grace for leaders integrating general prophetic ministry into the local church. While the prevalent use of prophetic ministry in evangelism, outreach, and other formats is completely legitimate and worthy of consideration, our primary focus is serving pastors in cultivating development contexts for the prophetic within the local church. Evangelism and outreach are excellent ministry formats that may include prophetic ministry, but prophecy is not typically the focus of these ministries. Also, while evangelism that includes prophetic ministry is addressed in many outstanding books, I wish to focus my efforts on developing prophetic ministry contexts within the local church at present.

1) Confidence Workshops

These are prophetic team ministry training environments where the gifts can be developed, feedback can be more direct and honest, and sensitivity can be honed through input.

This is the starting point for church-wide prophetic ministry development. It's also the team ministry starting line, allowing them to learn each others' tendencies in the Spirit, how others share their gifts, and working together to communicate His messages. I call them confidence workshops for the very reason that teams must learn to listen not only to the Spirit to gain confidence, but also to each other. This is the best way to train the members who will become a team.

As a team begins to take shape, it's best to have two types of workshops offered: One for the newly or casually interested members in the prophetic, where current members of the team can assist in training and teaching; and one for the more experienced members to work together and grow their sensitivity to the Spirit and each other. I would recommend that ministry over one another in development be recorded using phones and tablets for feedback on delivery, growth in clarity, and accountability for content.

Going Deeper in Creating Confidence Workshops

Confidence Workshops are leadership-planned meetings designed to equip and activate prophetic ministry in members.

If a pastor doesn't presently have proven, commissioned prophets in the church, or if they wish to oversee the development of the prophetic, they will need to teach and facilitate the gathering.

The objective is to build confidence in hearing God, sharing with one person or a group, while receiving some training and feedback in the process. God encouraged us to especially desire to prophesy (1 Cor. 14:1), so our pursuit of this confidence-building process is not presuming upon the spirit; it is obedience. We are always pursuing from a position of faith that God wants to speak to His people if we will listen.

We are not promoting a method or one way of building the ministry, as there are multiple ways to approach the development of this gift.

From the first meeting, the leadership team should be observing and pursuing members who demonstrate an increased capacity to prophesy in a consistent and accurate way. Faithful members in the church should be encouraged to share their knowledge, experience, and testimony of how God has taught them to use the gift.

It's very important to have people share testimonies about what God seems to be saying through other members, so those being used can be strengthened in their confidence.

A less formal setting may be appropriate for these workshops. I would suggest where possible that the group gather in a circle, having the leadership seated among the group. This can help the attendees sense that their involvement is important, and it lets them see it's less about teaching and more about doing.

Teaching should be kept as minimal as necessary, and I would suggest that the content be delivered in a question/answer/discussion environment as much as possible. By opening a dialog regarding the gift and its operation, the leadership team can get an immediate sense of each member's understanding and awareness of the gift.

When we get to the point in the workshop where it transitions to group or personal ministry, there are a few options to consider:

1) Have a brief time of worship singing so participants may sense what God might be saying or showing them for individuals or the group.

2) Encourage them to be precise and concise in their sharing to allow more ministry to occur, and to limit longer, more exhorting diatribes.

3) Have a period of prayer for the church, and working from that time, direct the participants to share what they feel God might be saying about the church. Remind them that we are looking for only what God is actually saying, not what they wish to add as their thoughts about what he's saying.

4) Break into groups of three, preferably with those members they don't know as well, and have two people prophesy over one. This two-on-one will continue until everyone in the small group has received ministry from the other two. I would encourage a time limit of the ministry to two to three minutes total, for each to share what they believe God has for the other person. For those who don't sense any words or pictures, they can pray briefly and be assured that God will faithfully respond to those prayers with prophetic insights.

These are all exercises of faith to create a sense of urgency to begin speaking rather than waiting until they get their thoughts together. Their own thoughts about what God is saying is something we want to limit in the flow.

None of these drills are intended to be a legalistic exercise, and I am not suggesting the time limit is somehow a biblical mandate. It's simply one means of grace to encourage faith and boldness in expressing the gift without trusting our own minds to work through everything before it's shared.

If the leadership chooses to give more time or not set a limit, that is fine, but the more that is shared, the more a person receiving has to sift through and remember.

Even if the ministry is recorded, the extended sharing can dilute the effectiveness of the ministry time substantially because the listener has to wade through it all for the part that God seems be saying. Additionally, there is more room for error when sharing is prolonged. Usually, the first part of what is shared is God, and the rest is trying to qualify and clarify His message. This isn't necessary if God is speaking. If clarification is needed, tell the person receiving ministry to ask for it when they are done being prayed over.

Prophecy originates from the Holy Spirit dwelling in us, but when the pure revelation passes through our minds, additional thoughts or stream of consciousness can hinder more than help.

During these exercises, I would suggest setting aside time to have testimonies about what God is doing. This greatly builds the faith of those who ministered, as well as the whole group. Increased confidence to prophesy is the goal, and testimonies immediately following ministry time are very effective tools to build faith.

For example, during the two-on-one session, you can have the person being ministered to share their experience during ministry before they move to the next person. This pause allows a momentary reset of each person's mind, builds faith for the next ministry moment, and encourages everyone if it's accurate.

It's not required for everyone to share their prophetic ministry experience, nor is it required for everyone to speak. We realize everyone is in a different place in their relationship with the Holy Spirit and the gifts, and each should feel the freedom to observe at their own pace, learn, and speak as they feel led. Everything should be done in faith, not under coercion, especially prophecy (Rom. 12:6, 14:23).

2) Care and Counseling Ministry

This is the first and most common area where prophetic ministry will be shared. During one-on-one prayer times and small group personal ministry moments, prophetic people are given the chance to strengthen their hearing and sharing with the help of the recipient's immediate feedback. This is also an excellent format for more experienced prophetic people to assist in providing feedback, examples, and training of other members. I would recommend that prophetic ministry over the church member(s) be recorded using phones and tablets for feedback on delivery, growth in clarity, and accountability for content.

3) Care (Small) Group Ministry

This could be corporately shared prophetic ministry to everyone in the care (small) group during worship and prayer times or the more formal manner of team ministry over individuals as invited by leadership.

This context would include any small group meetings organized by the church. It also represents a great test-bed for a fledgling prophetic ministry to be demonstrated and developed. It's a small group, so it will test the pride of those who believe they are called to something bigger, and it's a perfect size for those who are terrified, yet willing, to share what they feel God is saying through them.

This context provides one of the best environments to

edify, encourage, and comfort the believers in the local church. I would recommend that prophetic ministry over the church members be recorded using phones and tablets for feedback on delivery, growth in clarity, and accountability for content.

4) Corporate Ministry

Other church-organized meetings other than Sunday services, singles, youth, married couples, care group leaders, etc., are the next level of formal prophetic team ministry.

Requiring greater elder trust, the accountability and need for maturity is higher, and therefore it's imperative that the team be working together to only share what the Spirit says, without embellishments.

What the care group is to testing the individual prophetic gifts of team members, these smaller, yet more formal church group settings with elders present are excellent starting points for the entire prophetic team to develop and demonstrate their sphere of gifting.

Feedback is more immediate and helpful to the team, and the format is more relaxed. This allows the team to try different ways of delivering the ministry of the Spirit. Again, it's helpful to record audio and even video for feedback, growth, and accountability.

5) Congregational Ministry

This is the formal inclusion of the more experienced prophetic team members in ministry before the entire church, as invited by the elder team.

This is the biggest step in a local context for any prophetic ministry team. For this, the elder team's faith for prophetic ministry must be high. It's a bold, declarative statement of the elder team's commitment to the prophetic ministry. The team should consist of the most effective, proven, and mature prophetic team members.

This can also be done in an extra-local prophetic ministry opportunity at another church. This ratchets the leadership's faith and trust to stratospheric heights. The objective is never the team ministry's growth as a brand, but only that the church they serve is equipped and built up through their service. As always, record audio and video for feedback, growth, and accountability.

6) Conference Ministry

This would be the formal inclusion of team members, affirmed by local elder teams, ministering before multiple churches together, as invited by conference leadership.

This could be a proven local team, or a network presbytery of prophetic ministers coming together from different churches to serve. It's in this environment where only those with significant prophetic ministry gifts should be used, and only in contexts that serve the specific needs of the people present, as there is no higher accountability context.

There should be nothing done for show or entertainment purposes. Their involvement should be a faith building, edifying experience saturated with humility and the exaltation of Jesus Christ in every syllable spoken.

The presbytery, or networked prophetic members from different churches, should be led by a proven prophet or prophets, and the ministry should be closely supported and affirmed by elder pastors who know the prophetic members serving. At each level of service, we should record audio and video for feedback, growth, and accountability.

We don't wish to create these contexts as a ladder to be climbed in a prophetic ministry calling; rather we want to facilitate service with humility to the local church.

Positioning Prophetic Team Ministry Models as "Moments," Not Monuments to Men

Bring up the word *model*, and immediately the term *legalism* will crop up. Legalism in this context would be anything suggesting some set of actions as the only way ministry should be done to please God. We also want to avoid creating contexts that cultivate selfish ambition and build monuments to men.

As enthusiastic as I am in observing prophetic ministry moments in Scripture that give us great faith and hope that the Holy Spirit will do the same, or more, in our churches, we should be careful to maintain faith without creating overbearing rules or rituals. Consider instead prophetic "snapshots" in a widely varied photo album of Holy Spirit manifestations in the book of Acts.

While we certainly need glimpses into His ways to increase our expectation of Him, we must not raise our expectations or critique of others conforming to any sort of model drawn from the limited narrative in Acts. Due to the limited explanation given for the New Testament prophetic team ministry in these moments, we can only hope to gain basic insight into its function and service to the local church.

As much as we desire to serve pastors in providing insight, experience, and models to grow the prophetic team ministry based on Scripture and a calling to equip the Church, the Scripture is also filled with Pharisaical failures of building monuments to men, traditions, and rules. Therefore, we can only do our best to balance the clear doctrines of the Spirit from Scripture, with the experience He so faithfully provides to His Church.

The Holy Spirit intentionally limited the explanation of prophetic moments, so we are forced to be utterly dependent on Him for every breath of this ministry and its outworking, not looking to any one method or model. We are driven deeper into the Scripture and His presence to best understand what pleases Him in prophetically sharing His heart with others.

Also, it's so we don't make much of prophetic ministry or its structure; rather we ought to make much of Jesus, His gospel, His glory, and the building of His Church. If we then experience the privilege of having prophetic moments along the way, our focus will remain on Him, and not honoring men or women for their gifts, or our own way of doing things.

When the gracious and powerful Holy Spirit speaks to and through imperfect vessels through prophecy, it's not a stretch to expect temptations of pride, ambition, and self-promotion. If He uses team members in significant ways, it only becomes more important to surround those gifted members with a team to protect, pray, and provide connection to relationships, humility, and care.

Covering the acknowledged weakness of a member through the gathering of a team seeking to glorify God alone is a means of grace for any ministry team in the church. If there is any biblical model, it is of humility before, and dependence on, the Holy Spirit.

Chapter 11

Pondering Prophetic Moments in Scripture

D ue to the broad scope of pastoral experience, let's look at a few Church moments highlighted in Scripture that mirror the wide spectrum of different types of prophetic situations and attitudes toward prophecy that can arise in our churches. Some are actual prophetic moments, while others are examples for application to the prophetic for our purposes.

Examine these varied experiences not as a single way to pastor prophetic ministry; instead glean the best practices that the Holy Spirit may be prompting us to deploy in our local church. This leaves room for Him to encourage elder/leadership teams from many vantage points of experience without attempting to make a policy, or model, from any specific one.

Pastoring Prophetic Ministry in Optimal Conditions

Let's begin with a few Scriptural references to churches whose actions were an example we would recommend applying in the local prophetic team ministry context.

Berea — Eager and Examining

The Church at Berea was commended for searching the words of Paul to see if they were true. They held themselves accountable to confirm that what they were hearing was, in fact, God.

> "Now the Berean Jews were of more noble character than those in Thessalonica, for they received the message with great eagerness and examined the Scriptures every day to see if what Paul said was true. As a result, many of them believed." (Acts 17:11-12a NIV)

While this commendation was primarily focused on the Bereans' study of Paul's teaching, their commitment easily transfers to the need we have to be equally disciplined in our assessment of New Testament prophecy.

What the Bereans were hearing from Paul would have been a prophetic revelation to them and their eagerness to receive and review the messages against Scripture is an example of how we should be toward prophecies we receive today. The passage says that their enthusiastic pursuit resulted in greater numbers of true believers. This faith-building outcome from their diligence is what we desire for every church.

> "Consider carefully what you hear," he continued. "With the measure you use, it will be measured to you—and even more. Whoever has will be given more; whoever does not have, even what they have will be taken from them." (Mark 4:24 NIV)

A dear friend, pastor, and brother in the faith, Pat McGuffin, pointed me to the application of this verse in Mark 4:24, where Jesus exhorts those with ears to hear what He's communicating about the kingdom of God and to not ignore it. Jesus gives a promise and sober warning to "consider carefully" what they are hearing, and not to take it for granted. He encourages those who are faithful to respond eagerly to what they are hearing with a promise of more. Those who don't have this posture are told they will experience a drift away from the perspective they currently possess.

Applying this broadly to the Holy Spirit's pursuit of our hearts, both prophetically and personally, there doesn't appear to be a neutral position with regard to our response to Him. To those who have eager "ears to hear" and respond obediently, He will give more. More insight personally, and more prompting prophetically.

To those who are reticent to receive from Him, regardless of their reasons, there appears to be some sort of withdrawal made regarding that person's understanding of these things ("... what they have will be taken from them" Mark 4:24). I would expect from other descriptions in Scripture of drift away from the Spirit that this could include a hardening of the heart to His ongoing work in the Church ("Today if you hear his voice, do not harden your hearts." Heb. 4:7).

My intent is to exhort all of us to allow the Holy Spirit continuing access to our hearts prophetically and personally, to engage a Berean discipline of eagerness and examination with all we believe we are hearing. This exhortation has the local church elder team clearly in view. For any prophetic team ministry to grow, they must also be considering carefully how the Holy Spirit is speaking to them about it.

The goal is to increase faith for more of what God speaks to us, His Church, both through the Scriptures and prophecy. To freshly inspire some who may have grown weary or been hardened by unfortunate experience, limited doctrine, or no experience at all, I say, revisit your willingness to be eager, and examine what the Holy Spirit seems to be saying to you and the Church through prophecy.

Antioch—Equipping and Encouraging

All of the significant narrative moments in the book of Acts regarding prophecy and prophets centered around the Church at Antioch. It's not clear from Scripture why Antioch received this distinction, but I believe it was a newly formed gentile church in great need of encouragement, edification, and comfort. During their early years they experienced seasons of great disagreement among the apostles and Pharisees of the day about circumcision and polity in the new work the Holy Spirit was doing in the

Church (Acts 15:1-35). Despite the Church's challenges in its early days, we observe a series of prophetic moments that form a compelling overview of how this ministry can serve everyday Church life.

While prophets were resident in Antioch (Acts 13:1), two of the three events mentioned in these verses regarding this church included mention of prophetic teams sent from Jerusalem (Acts 11:27, 15:32). This speaks to Antioch's openness to prophetic ministry from proven, trusted churches outside their congregation to build up their church.

They were not only seeing prophetic ministry occur within the Church, but they were pursuing prophetic ministry from Jerusalem. We can point to Antioch as a picture of a humble, hungry Church with leaders who welcomed the trustworthy work of the Holy Spirit from within (Acts 13:1-3), and without (Acts 11:27, Acts 15:32).

It's ironic that during this five-chapter section of Scripture, Acts 11-15, where the most disagreement over early Church function, polity, and legalism surrounding the Gentiles was recorded, that the most profound moments of New Testament prophecy were captured.

The irony is that prophecy, a revelatory gift, as doctrinally divisive as it is today, was a unifying means of grace during a divisive time in the early Church. The Holy Spirit sent the prophetic to encourage, strengthen, and sustain the Church through that season.

This is what we should be seeking in the prophetic today. Despite the endless argument in the Church about function, polity, and legalism, the prophetic should be a continuing, unifying beacon of encouragement, edification, and comfort to its leaders and members.

If this was a reason why the prophetic was so active and important during that season of the Antioch Church, we could not only miss the kindness of God to Antioch, but also to our local churches. We could focus so much on the right church model, as the apostles were doing, in trying to fit Antioch into their view of Christendom at that time that we could be in danger of missing the faithful moments of ministry from the Holy Spirit to prophetically build up the Church.

While the Church leadership in Jerusalem was arguing about the model (Acts 11), the prophetic was serving the Church (Agabus in Acts 11:28), the leadership (Acts 13:1-4), and the individuals (Judas and Silas in Acts 15). We must not spend our time striving over the perfect model for prophetic ministry, but encourage its use for the equipping and building up of the body of Christ.

> *This is the value of true prophetic ministry in the local church: It serves to strengthen the hearts of the people when the circumstances of their lives no longer can.* —Lewis Seifert

Prophetic Protocol in Delivery

In light of the Spirit's ongoing kindness to Antioch, we should consider carefully how the prophetic was one significant way He chose to express that kindness to them. Our faith should be bolstered for the prophetic in our local churches by His faithfulness to Antioch.

While He uses an economy of words and limits each explanation, the Holy Spirit clearly manifests three different types of prophetic ministry that produced significant fruit in the local church. Each of them should become something elder teams everywhere are asking Him to repeat in their meetings for the sake of His Church and His glory.

1) Congregational prophetic ministry

Agabus predicts a famine (Acts 11:27-28)

Agabus was uniquely gifted as a prophet in the New Testament, and in the realm of prediction (Acts 11:28, 21:11). In this passage, he was visiting Antioch with a prophetic team sent from Jerusalem. He stood up in the midst of the church and declared what the Holy Spirit was saying to him. We don't have the number of people he addressed, but this appears to be a corporately shared prophetic utterance with a substantial predictive element.

The point here is not the significance of the prediction he gave, but the context and manner in which it was delivered (corporately and concisely) before the church. It's also significant how the church elders responded. It was a prophetic word that was received with such faith that it produced unity and generosity among all the believers to assist those who would be in need. Whenever a prophetic utterance brings faith, unity, and generosity in believers on this scale, it's a clear sign and validation of the gift that God is among His people and working.

2) Prophetic ministry serving leadership

"Prophets and teachers...Set apart for me..." (Acts 13:1-2)

This passage demonstrates the unique relationship that exists between prophets and teachers in the New Testament. While the passage listed the names of the prophets and teachers, none of them were attributed for prophesying the Holy Spirit's command to "Set apart for me Barnabas and Saul" (Acts 13:2)

The significance of omitting the name of the prophet, from a team ministry perspective, is that it doesn't matter who said what. What matters is that the message was delivered amidst unity between the prophets and teachers, stated clearly for all present, and offered in a timely fashion so they could pray and commission Paul and Barnabas. It wasn't about who got credit for hearing and speaking; it was about the Holy Spirit using His prophetic servants to serve the elder team to validate and separate those men for His purpose.

Antioch humbly received prophetic ministers from Jerusalem (Acts 11:27, 15:32) on multiple occasions. The Holy Spirit used these visiting ministers to develop prophets who were present in Antioch as part of the church when He launched Paul, one of the most prolific ministers in history (Acts 13:1-3). They went from being a church having ministry gifts sent to them, to being a church that sent ministry gifts all over the world. This is the power of imparting, faith-building prophetic ministry operating by the Holy Spirit in a God-honoring way in the local church.

Antioch: A Metaphor for Balanced Ministry

The presence of prophets and teachers worshiping the Lord and fasting together implies that the priority was the Church and unity among the leaders, not labels or authority. In Acts 13, we are told that there were prophets and teachers in Antioch. At first glance, it appears there is a perfunctory identification of two groups of gifted men seeking the Lord: the teachers, who are committed to doctrinal accuracy and interpretation, and the prophets, who hear God's voice and share what they feel He is saying to the Church. This is a strong metaphor for the juxtaposition of doctrine and experience in the local church.

Some say doctrine is all we need for life and godliness and that experience is shallow, over-rated, and not to be trusted. There are those who prefer experience over the value of sound doctrine in their relationship with the Holy Spirit, feeling that too much emphasis on doctrine will hinder faith for what God might do because it encourages an increasing trust in traditions.

This doctrine/experience debate has raged for centuries in the Church, and in a few simple sentences the Holy Spirit demonstrates His pleasure when these two representatives of the argument become united in one Church, at one time, for one purpose. Out of this unity in Antioch, it's significant that He launches Paul, the most prolific church planter and Scripture writer of the entire New Testament, into His ministry.

There was a willingness to seek God together for His will, evident in their relationships, worship, and fasting for the Lord's presence. Relationship, worship, and fasting are all vulnerable and dependent actions toward the Lord, indicating that there wasn't a tension over roles and responsibilities, or Doctrine vs. Experience, only a passion for His direction for their church.

The only tension that existed around Antioch at that time had nothing to do with prophecy, but rather how the Gentiles would be included in the family of New Testament churches and what stipulations, if any, would be put on them (Acts 15).

This was not a one-time gathering of leaders; these men had been together for some time before this event is highlighted (Acts 11:25-26). There was a oneness in their doctrine and experience that should inspire men in leadership.

The manifestation of the Holy Spirit of God through a local church of unity, faith, and release of the gifts to the world should be a part of every church. Antioch is an excellent moment that esteems unification of the leadership gifts, balancing doctrine and experience on the fulcrum of the gospel. This will happen in local churches where pastors and teachers have sought to value other leadership gifts operating in their midst and to see them raised up to function alongside them for the ministry and maturing of the Body of Christ.

3) Prophetic Team Ministry Serving the Local Church

Judas and Silas encouraged the brothers (Acts 15:32)

From the initial evangelistic push upon his arrival, to

engaging Paul's help in the teaching ministry, Barnabas was the quintessential team player in Antioch. It says He was a "good man, full of the Holy Spirit, and of faith" (Acts 11:24). His manner seems evident in the ongoing team ministry occurring in Antioch through other good men, full of the Holy Spirit, and of faith

Two such men, Judas and Silas, "who were themselves prophets" (Acts 15:32), were added to a delegation sent from the apostles in Jerusalem to encourage the Church. These two men were used in team prophetic ministry just as all the prophetic ministry had been prior to their arrival. This pattern of a plural use of the word "prophets" in Acts 11:27, 13:1, and 15:32 is evidence that, like Old Testament prophets before them, they found working together was a much more effective means of ministry than alone.

Team ministry was Jesus' idea. In Luke 10:1, when He sent out the seventy-two, He sent them "two by two." He understood the value of people working together. He understood the encouragement, boldness, and support of a team setting.

This team approach was to continue, by command of the Holy Spirit, in Acts 13:2 when He instructed the teachers and prophets gathered in prayer at Antioch to, "set apart for me Barnabas and Saul for the work to which I have called them."

Also, Antioch was a gentile church plant that the Jerusalem church heavily supported, with various leaders sent to care for its growth. They sent apostles, evangelists, and two prophets to serve the local church. Identifying their callings isn't about rank or highlighting the importance of the men, but rather the pattern of the Holy Spirit in supporting churches with team ministry through gifted men called to the Church.

This is how New Testament prophetic ministry should operate corporately, both to the leadership, and individually in today's Church.

Prophetic ministry has become a divisive issue, rising from the concern over new revelation and the closed canon. The Holy Spirit shows us through Antioch that despite doctrinal disagreement over issues, prophecy should be a fountain of unification, confirmation, and edification of God's rich presence working mightily among us, in us, and through us to His glory.

Chapter 12

Prophetic Ministry in More Enthusiastic Conditions

While Berea and Antioch provide examples and moments in the Holy Spirit that could easily populate any elder team's prayer list, there are other church moments that needed adjustment, which reveal similar challenges pastors face in developing prophetic ministry.

The first and most notable church needing adjustment was Corinth. When elder teams open the door to corporate prophecy and developing prophetic team ministry, it's likely they will encounter extremely enthusiastic members with some of the attributes of the Corinthians.

It's critical to state before we explore this example that Paul never sought to use Corinth as a reason to diminish prophecy, but rather he sought to create protocols for it to flourish even more. It's my prayer that elder teams take the same faith-filled, patient view of those members in their churches who tend toward a Corinthian approach to prophecy and the gifts.

Corinth

It's in these letters from Paul to the Church at Corinth that the most obvious descriptions of unrestrained spiritual experiences occur in the gathering of believers. According to 1 Corinthians 14, it appears the spiritual gifts, and primarily tongues, were manifesting in some disorderly way during their meetings.

The sense we get from the corrections being offered by Paul suggests that there was a lot of talking over one another, confusion from the unbridled use of tongues, and attempting to interrupt each other in the use of the gifts during corporate gatherings. Because Paul called for it in the last verse of the chapter, it is clear that the Church lacked decency and order.

In a number of today's charismatic churches, the same could be said for their services that lack order and decency, draw attention to men, and leave attendees wondering if it was God, more than having a wonder *for* God.

There can be a reticence toward the spiritual gifts in many pastors who feel things get too out of hand for God to be honored properly. In attempting to protect the flock, they delete most, if not all, of these expressions to ensure no one is exposed unnecessarily to excess or a bad experience.

For any number of reasons ranging from doctrinal positions, to poor experience, to no experience, they can take the 1 Corinthians 14:40 command that says we should do everything "decently and in order" and reword it to say we should see everything as "discontinued to restore order."

This limited approach to inclusion of the Spirit's gifts to reduce confusion and congregational awkwardness has led many leaders to adopt a new term: *continuationists*.

They still believe in the value of the person and work of the Holy Spirit and His gifts, but their desire not to be labeled as *charismatics* stems from how they feel the Holy Spirit is so poorly portrayed in those meetings.

While I understand the tension that exists for leaders, Paul never condemned the Corinthian Church's pursuit of the gifts, just their lack of protocol. Free-for-all must cease, but vocal and revelatory gifts in the Church today should not cease.

Despite the debate over service decorum and discipline continuing, as it relates to prophetic utterance and its use in Church today, we are forever admonished by Paul to eagerly desire it and not to forsake it (1 Cor. 14:1; 1 Thess. 5:19).

While we may not have an entire church like Corinth, and we will do all we can to avoid it, we may have members with enthusiasm that manifest in shades of Corinth. Enthusiasm's Greek roots are *en* and *theos*, or "of God," which suggests that the presence of excitement for the prophetic gift should not be thwarted in any way, only the manner in which it's ministered. It takes great skill in a pastor to not reduce enthusiasm as they attempt to mature a gift of prophecy.

I would encourage an elder to review his own heart regarding enthusiastic prophetic members who seem to have a gift but are annoying in their manner or delivery. Personal preference isn't always helpful in discerning what needs correction in the enthusiastic person. If prophecy is done decently and in order and the only issue is personality attributes, can you be confident your concern is shared by the Holy Spirit? If not, the annoying manner is the Spirit's job to correct.

I was a very enthusiastic prophetic member who needed regular correction and adjustment to my pride and ambition. My failures manifested mostly in a lack of love and patience when I spoke. The messages were accurate for the most part, but the delivery was not edifying because of my immaturity and personal challenges.

Paul's gracious and faith-filled handling of Corinth should be a road map to how we develop the gifts, and especially the prophetic in our people. He bookends the chapters dealing with the gifts and the command to eagerly desire, which includes prophecy (1 Cor. 12 and 14), with an exhortation that everything be done in love, decently, and in order. Everything else is about reducing confusion and building up the Church through providing clarity, parsing opportunity, and promoting assessment.

This is not a debate nor discourse on the validity of different spiritual experiences. It's clear the Holy Spirit was willing to manifest in Corinth despite the issues of distraction that arose. He knows we are just children. The plea for decency and order by Paul wasn't to shut down their pursuit of the spiritual gifts, but rather to create contexts for it to properly edify the Church as intended. Paul reinforced their desire for spiritual manifestations, but at the same time repositioned the purpose and protocol to produce greater fruit.

Prophetic Delivery Protocol for More Enthusiastic Members

Outward physical manifestations, such as shaking, head bobbing, voice quiver, and significant crying, in the one prophesying is not a measure, nor sign, of more anointing; it's more likely a distraction to the hearer. There is no biblical validation of overly self-promoting expressive actions performed while prophesying, unless they were used as part of the prophecy itself (Agabus binding his hands and feet in Acts 21:11).

Therefore, my brothers and sisters, be eager to prophesy, and do not forbid speaking in tongues. But everything should be "done in a fitting and orderly way" (1 Cor. 14:39-40 NIV). The English Standard Version says everything should be "done decently and in order."

1)   *The spirit of the prophet is subject to, or under the control of, the prophet (1 Cor. 14:32-33)*

The prophetic person needs to deliver their message decently and in order for the purpose of edifying the Church. Significant shows of dramatic emotion, action, or voice inflections can be unhelpful and seem self-serving.

2)   *The glory of the prophetic moment is to declare God's manifest presence among us, not draw attention to our being used.*

The drawing of undue attention to one's self instead of to whom it's rightly due, the triune God, is not only inappropriate, but also a dangerous practice.

3)   *Prophecy is a vocal expression in a corporate setting.*

The Spirit primarily manifests through our breath, not our body. We must strive to restrain anything that might distract the person(s) receiving the message from God through us.

Suggestions for Working with Extremely Enthusiastic Prophetic Persons

It's critical that the elder team give timely feedback to enthusiastic prophetic members, especially those who prophesy on a corporate level. It's not enough that they heard God and shared His message; the affirmation of leadership for the accuracy and assurance of their ministry is important as well.

Prophetic ministry is done "through a glass, darkly" (1 Cor. 13:12 KJV), and while it can sound confident, especially from the enthusiastic person, the elders must divine what the prophetic people need. It would help them to draw on their own need for feedback in preaching. To preach a message with little to no feedback would be challenging, and so it is for the prophetic person as well.

1)   *Identify those causing issues and confront them lovingly.*

If they are responding to correction, trust the Holy Spirit to develop their character and gift. If they don't respond to correction or input, then they need to step back from ministry.

2)   *Keep a close eye on each prophetic person's family relationships and keep them accountable.*

Prophetic individuals can lose sight of personal growth in pursuit of the prophetic. This was always a focus of my own pastor's pursuit of my heart, and it served me very well in my growth in the prophetic and in character.

3)   *Provide clear guidelines for how ministry should be done when the Spirit is moving.*

Share the protocol and requirement for accountability with your team. Remind them that the spirits of the prophets are subject to the prophets in ministry times (1 Cor. 14:32) and that everything should be done decently and in order for the building up of the Church. (1 Cor. 14:40).

4)   Setup a ministry microphone managed by an elder and/or prophet who will work with those coming to share in any corporate gatherings.

This provides an intermediate step of humility for the member, submitting what they believe they are hearing before it's shared. This will challenge them to prepare more precisely and concisely what they plan to say. It's common for young prophets to speak longer than they should; this will help tighten it up. Also, are there any doctrinal concerns that need to be addressed as well?

5)   Always affirm them by continuing to encourage their faith for the gifts, as Paul did.

There is no reason to diminish faith if they haven't perfected sharing the message yet. As long as they are willing to submit to oversight and accountability, they should be receiving encouragement to continue.

6)   Handle miscues as individual occurrences and reduce any tendency toward a categorical dismissal of the gift as "too messy."

It's inevitable that members who are more enthusiastic will miss it from time to time, and therefore it's important for the elder team to respond swiftly and patiently by directing their attention to the error, any verses in the Bible that might support the correction, and provide counsel on any restoration or forgiveness that needs to be pursued.

7)   Encourage what God brings through them as much as possible, so they know the elder team is still in faith for them.

They may be gifted of God, yet struggle in social settings to see the necessary attitudes that best serve the church. They will be more responsive if they believe the elder team sees gifting, even if it is limited in maturity and character.

8) *Address it if their personal prophetic ministry causes concerns in other members.*

It's important to keep the correction focused on the specific areas needed for growth, so they don't always feel they are being singled out for adjustment. Some members have personality preferences when receiving ministry and that must not cloud the elder team's judgment in what needs true correction in the offending member.

9) *If their delivery is awkward, loud, overly fast, or filled with attempts to sound eloquent, point them back to the importance of authenticity and humility.*

We should be bold, but there should not be a significant difference in the person's delivery from their normal speech pattern except in confidence and greater volume. Strange movements, odd voice inflections, or flutters fall under the exhortation to self-control, which is a fruit of the Spirit (Gal. 5:22).

10) *Provide a reasonable number of meeting contexts for faith-filled people to grow and be used prophetically.*

The elder team must not avoid those with enthusiastic prophetic gifts, but rather provide structured environments for them to be grown and matured. Ignoring them and hoping they will get a clue could lead to them becoming discouraged or bitter, the opposite of what timely correction should do.

11) *Build a relationship with extra-local pastors who have experience in working with prophetic people, to provide encouragement, wisdom, and guidance.*

This is an invaluable resource in remaining true to what God may be doing to redeem a difficult situation with a member who needs to mature in the use of the gift.

12)   Bring in a trusted, proven prophetic team to assist in equipping and training those with faith to grow.

Having the support of prophetic people who have more experience and maturity can be very helpful in assisting challenging members to understand their need to serve the Church, not be served.

13)   Provide prophetic training resources from trusted, proven gift ministries that can assist in changing perspectives for those who feel the elder team isn't as "in faith" for the prophetic as they are.

Having regular access to leaders to discuss these resources, even if it's just through email and phone conversations, will go a long way to dispel the prophetic person's sense that the leadership team is unresponsive or uncaring toward them and their gift.

Chapter 13

Prophetic Ministry in Less Enthusiastic Conditions

If an elder team is more inclined to develop a prophetic team than the members are to participate, this presents a different set of challenges for the pastors. In any context where indifference may be present, the first priority is to stir passion for the person of Jesus Christ and His Church.

When members are comfortable in their routines and patterns, the Holy Spirit will stir up their faith afresh for more of what He wishes to do in and through them. Pastors have a daunting task in drawing people out of this indifferent state into one that invites the Holy Spirit to have His way in them.

This description may not involve the entire church fellowship, only those who dabble in the gifts, with the faith to step up. Pastors may see great things God wants to do with certain people prophetically and personally, and with a little encouragement and discipleship, they may become warriors in the kingdom of God. Let's look at how we can address the less enthusiastic members through the lens of the Church at Laodicea.

Laodicea

I know your deeds, that you are neither cold nor hot. I wish you were either one or the other! So, because you are lukewarm--neither hot nor cold—I am about to spit you out of my mouth. You say, 'I am rich; I have acquired wealth and do not need a thing.' But you do not realize that you are wretched, pitiful, poor, blind and naked...Those whom I love I rebuke and discipline. So be earnest and repent. Here I am! I stand at the door and knock. If anyone hears my voice and opens the door, I will come in and eat with that person, and they with me. (Rev. 3:14-17, 19-20 NIV)

The challenge of leading indifferent believers is particularly difficult. This is usually evidence of self-sufficiency, unbelief, and pride. ("You say, 'I am rich; I have acquired wealth and do not need a thing.'")

For the prophetic to grow in a Laodicean environment, it will require a revival ignited by the gospel and Holy Spirit in the lives of the unrecognized called. It's the gospel that freshly awakens our deep need for the Holy Spirit and His work.

It will also require times of intentional pursuit of intimacy in worship and corporate prayer by the church. These times usually lead to repentance and a fresh outpouring of His love on His people. It's during these intentional pursuits that the pastor can invite those who desire to grow in this gift to find fresh faith to be used. It will feel to the pastor that they are having to prime a pump at first, but God is always faithful to stir His people when the leaders direct them back to Jesus.

For those lost in a Laodicean mindset toward the Spirit, pastoral initiation is a powerful force for faith to be activated in the people. It's not manipulating emotion, or charismatic cheerleading; it's the Spirit responding to the authority of the local elder team on behalf of the church. He will respond with a spirit of prophecy in the meeting. This spirit of prophecy activates all levels of prophetic ministry present in the room and often leads to wonderful times of ministry.

The elder team will need to be willing to step out in this faith-building context of pastoral initiation in any setting where the prophetic people are present and the church is gathered. There is no limit on the Spirit's work and timing toward His people. It's the pastors who hold a significant key to unlock the blessing of the Holy Spirit on their people through the prophetic ministry.

Prophetic Delivery Protocol for Less Enthusiastic Members

Members who are less outgoing at the start may struggle in communicating prophetic ministry in a corporate setting. All are to be reminded that corporate ministry is only one of many ways the Holy Spirit can work through them. They should certainly not feel pressured or expected to always prophesy in a corporate setting. There are many other contexts where they can effectively and faithfully serve God in the prophetic without ever speaking before the Church.

If we have less enthusiastic or low-key members who do wish to prophesy corporately, here are a few things to make sure they understand:

1)   *When the Spirit fills a person to be used, it's usually accompanied by a boldness of speech* (Acts 4:31)

   This doesn't mean they must yell, but they should speak in a confident and clear manner, with energy consistent with the infilling of the Spirit.

2)   *They don't have to explain everything about any picture or vision they are receiving, and they don't have to speak for a long time to be prophetic.*

   A good practice for people who are sharing for the first few times is to have them write the word down for submission and review. This provides a simple assessment platform, while easing the pressure to speak extemporaneously.

3)   *They need to avoid using repetitive terms or phrases and pausing midstream with "ums" and "uhs."*

   Encourage them to take their time, speak clearly, and avoid nervous ticks common to those who struggle with speaking publicly. In a smaller setting, it's appropriate to encourage them to pause and take their time.

4)   *It may be helpful for the elder to stand next to them or nearby while they share.*

While there, the elder can respond to the message as it is shared with encouraging expressions and words, such as, "Good," "Thank you, Lord," "Yes, very helpful." These affirming words shared sincerely and quietly during the pauses of the message where only the speaker can hear greatly encourage their confidence and boldness to speak.

I recall many instances in my own experience when I would hear the faith-filled vocal support of one of my pastors standing nearby, and it never failed to bolster my sharing in the moment.

5)   *Remind them of Paul's words to the Corinthians regarding his speech issues.*

In 1 Cor. 2:4 (NIV) Paul says, "My message and my preaching were not with wise and persuasive words, but with a demonstration of the Spirit's power." Those who are overly self-conscious or performance-oriented in their assessment will benefit greatly from this verse. They must not be anxious about their weakness of speech, but rather focused on the power of the Spirit within them.

All who minister prophetically must remember that the only thing that makes our words "prophecy" is the Holy Spirit's active, manifest presence in our midst.

Suggestions for Discipling Less Enthusiastic Prophetic Persons:

1)   *There must be a season of building fresh vision for an increasing work of the Spirit through teaching and encouragement in the doctrines of the Holy Spirit.*

It's not about trying to work up an experience, but

rather building faith for God to move afresh on the Church. It's important for pastors to regularly draw attention to the ongoing work of the Spirit and the members' need to keep in step with what He is doing.

2)   *Create non-threatening contexts for people to share what they are hearing, to build their faith.*

In addition to the suggestions already made, pastors will need to walk their mildly interested members through self-doubt and defeat, en route to confidence born of the gospel and grace flowing from the Holy Spirit working within them. Creating meeting contexts will help immensely in this process.

3)   *Encourage interested prophetic members to meet for fifteen minutes prior to the start of the main service to share what they believe God may be giving them and to pray about what He might be doing.*

This provides yet another intermediate step of building confidence before having to "go public" with what they hear.

4)   *Encourage prophetic ministry and worship in care groups for growth of the gifts.*

Directly challenge these members to use their gifts in their care group settings to build confidence and growth. Have the leaders support the request by drawing those specific prophetic members into prayer times and ministry moments in the group.

5)   *Encourage the most willing of the prophetically motivated to reach out to those God may put on their hearts for stirring and discipleship.*

A respected member encouraging the meek will build leadership in the encourager and confidence in the encouraged.

*6)   Create contexts for gifted prophetic members to pray for the
less enthusiastic ones, with an emphasis on impartation.*

Communicate the elder team's faith to grow this
ministry in the church and the desire to see people raised
up, and then have them prayed over to see what God may
have for them.

*7)   Setting up prophetic team ministry over specific candidates
to create a context for hearing God speak about what He is
doing to raise up individuals (Prophetic Presbytery).*

This can include bringing in prophetic individuals
from other churches and/or selecting proven gifts within
the church and having them join the local leadership team
to pray for key people who are candidates for ministry
(Acts 13:1-3; 1 Tim 4:14).

*8)   The elder team could bring in a prophetic team to
demonstrate and facilitate training and faith from outside
church.*

This experience could greatly envision the members
and build their faith for God to use them in a similar way
to the serve their local church.

Part 3: The Messengers of Prophecy

Introduction to Part 3

DISCIPLESHIP - *Who are we training in the prophetic ministry and how?*

Discipleship is the mentoring application of grace for growth in another believer.

Pastors are about discipleship. Speaking about prophetic team ministry growth in this context should be a language leaders understand.

In the Old Testament, God used the wilderness, caves, and a simple life to hone His prophetic messengers into teams. In the New Testament He is using the local church as a type of wilderness to develop His prophetic messengers and teams. The wilderness model for the New Testament is a challenge of discipleship through relationships in the local church.

Pastors provide mission-critical support to this process through ongoing care (discipling), accountability (character), and teaching (preaching). In this next section we seek to better understand how God develops the messengers of prophecy through the pastor in discipleship relationships.

Chapter 14

Understanding and Discipling the Messengers

B eing a disciple of Jesus Christ is the foremost calling of every prophetic believer. The details may vary greatly, but discipleship is a fixed point in New Testament Holy Spirit experience. Discipleship is similar to the Old Testament prophetic experience of mentoring that occurred between older and younger prophets. Made possible by the Spirit's presence, discipleship unto Christ-likeness is our loving response to the Father as evidenced by faithfulness. We praise the Father for possessing it toward us, as we seek to be faithful toward Him. Faithfulness in discipleship is the measure of our affection for the Father. Pastors should look for faithfulness when identifying prophetic team members.

Faithfulness and Gifting

And what you have heard from me in the presence of many witnesses entrust to faithful men who will be able to teach others also. (2 Tim. 2:2)

At the core of any true disciple of Jesus Christ is faithfulness to the Father and His Church. According to the dictionary, *faithfulness* is being "true to the original." Whether in failure or success, hardship or holiness, there is an undeniable authenticity of spirit and motive to the original truth of the gospel.

Degree of gifting can expand, depth of knowledge can grow, ability to lead can improve, but it's a prophetic person's integrity of love and loyalty in serving the local church that will determine their genuineness. There should certainly be an evident desire and maturing capacity for the gift of prophecy, but the primary assessment for team inclusion should be faithfulness.

This is the starting point for determining who the core members of the prophetic ministry team will be in the local church. Jesus never measured a man's talent, gifts, or outward actions as that which defined him; He weighed their faithfulness. In John 14:15, he says, "If you love me, you will keep my commandments." It was surrender and service to His will that He declared as true love for Him.

Faithfulness, as an authentic disposition of the heart in a prophetic person, should offset mistakes, pride, and immaturity. Faithfulness will be evident in their personal life, commitment to the gospel message, impartation through their life and teaching, and maturity in not being tossed about by every wind of doctrine.

It's more than just a Sunday expression at a microphone; it's carrying the Church in their heart, in their gift, and in their life. They are active in multiple contexts and meetings, with a consistent desire to care, impart, teach, lead, and serve the body with their gift. And in their life, while there may be things that need to be adjusted in delivery, manner, character, and doctrine, there is no mistaking their passion for the local church in how they serve others with what God gives them.

This is the test of our generation before God. Will we be faithful with the stewardship God has given us, to pass along a genuine demonstration of this gift to the next generation? If we are not the final generation of Christ's return, then we will be assessed for our faithfulness to the call of equipping, building, and maturing the body of Christ.

Discipling Prophetic Ministry by Understanding Each Other Better

Pastors inspired to reach out will be tempted to think, if

they don't already, that some of these prophetic people are sort of...well...weird.

As pastors choose to love their prophetic people and get to know them, they will likely discover many wonderful aspects of these odd people's personalities that they didn't understand when they were drawing prior conclusions.

The following descriptions are meant to grow awareness of typical prophetic tendencies. I have drawn this list from years of local church prophetic ministry experience, including my own failures.

While the focus may lean toward the weaknesses pastors will face in their prophetic people, remember that this entire book is designed to reinforce prophetic ministry's capacity by the Spirit to bring great encouragement to the Church. Don't allow this concentration of potential issues cause you to miss all that God has for us.

What pastors need to know about, or can expect from prophetic people and...

...their gift ministry/delivery to the church...

Prophetic people sometimes miss the point that a loving delivery is more important than a lofty revelation. Hold them accountable with all grace and kindness.

Without love, prophecy is nothing, a clanging cymbal (1 Cor. 13:1). It's the spirit of the prophet that is as important as the message they bring.

The fruit of the Spirit must richly flow from the heart of the prophetic person to ensure the greatest amount of anointing. A preoccupation with accuracy, volume, or opportunity can easily sidetrack the prophetic person from the much more important nature of their delivery.

The presence of the fruit of the Spirit powerfully validates the content of any prophetic message, and it severely reduces the likelihood of collateral damage.

Prophetic people often quickly cut to the heart of a matter, without building emotional bridges first, and this can lead to misunderstanding and offense in others.

Prophetic people have little patience for arguments about peripheral issues. They will want to get straight to the heart and motive of the matter. They believe that authenticity in discussion of the things of God should include a healthy attitude of self-discovery, assessment, and confession. Working through all the possibilities, listening with empathy, and seeking to understand others' feelings is not typically a strength.

Like a husband who believes the answer for his wife lies in solving her problem and not listening to her, prophetic people lead with the truth as they see it and expect a grateful response to what they share. Because they know the truth will set people free, they see no reason to remain silent when the answer is so obvious to them.

Prophetic people can end up making the proverbial mountain out of a molehill. Their direct, black-and-white and universal application of truth to a situation suggests they are out of touch with reality, lack common sense, or don't wish to face simple truths. This approach can be very frustrating to teachers, compassionate realists, and those unfamiliar with prophetic people in general.

They may be right in some way, but wrong in their awareness of harshness and insensitivity, thus nullifying their message.

Pastors must help prophetic people understand that God reveals the truth that sets people free, and only He can open the eyes of the blind. No amount of clanging the cymbal of loveless prophetic ministry can produce one iota of change or repentance. It's His kindness that leads men to repentance, and pastors need to help prophetic people understand this kindness through their example. They do this by handling the prophetic person's voracious self-righteousness the same way God dealt with theirs, with patience and kindness leading to repentance.

Prophetic people may hear the voice of God, but their interpretation and application can still be immature. Provide gentle, honest feedback with faith.

Because of their Spirit-heightened imagination, mental acuity, and empathic sensitivity to His prompting, they can "sync" more readily to what the Spirit seems to be saying for a situation or person. However, these God-breathed "upgrades" installed in a flawed human being can be a unique burden for pastors.

The burden is in the beauty of God's grace manifesting powerfully to encourage His Church, against the weakness of the person's undeveloped character to interpret and biblically apply what they are hearing.

Leadership should persist in faith for God to use such individuals for the Church, while dealing with the collateral damage of confused content, presumed contexts, and assumed conditions in the development process.

Confused content might be a misinterpretation of the message as it's shared or the right ideas shared with too many words. Presumed context is either a right message shared with the wrong person or it's the right message, right person, but applied in the wrong area of their life. Assumed conditions is either a right message shared with added legalistic expectations for the word to come to pass or it's an incomplete message that leaves out Spirit-directed expectations because of the fear of man or seeking approval.

Prophecy is a gift requiring stewardship, maturity, and discipline. Church leadership must provide active accountability with great encouragement to inspire meaningful growth.

In the absence of elder support, prophetic ministry can become presumptuous or harsh due to the speaker's struggles with being ignored or unappreciated. Conversely, in the absence of encouragement to grow their gifts, prophetic ministry can also be ignored and avoided by the gifted person.

Whichever the case, it's up to the leaders to embrace the gift's presence by encouraging faith to speak while holding the ministry accountable to help it grow in its value to the church.

Prophetic people are prone to irritation and anger at injustice, unrighteousness, and inconsistency. Diligently adjust self-righteousness while preserving relationship.

Prophetic people have a keen eye for sin. If they are godly, they will see their own sin as worse than what they observe elsewhere.

Nonetheless, they easily spot things that are not right. They tend to have a difficult time constraining their anger at these failures in others. This anger can, at times, be a righteous one, but that would only be for a moment to address something in a redemptive way. Anger is permitted, but it must be without sin (Eph. 4:26).

Anger that leads to sin in prophetic people can often stem from a lingering irritation at themselves. They are projecting frustration toward their own treacherous heart into their criticism of others.

Also, their anger can stem from their frustration with God, regarding His timing in their own lives. Their impatience with God's plan can lead to harshness toward others that they may or may not be able to see in themselves.

At Freedom Fellowship, during a prophetic training program I attended in October 2014, my prophet friend, Dr. Ray Self, said, "We prophesy on this side of the cross." Jesus took all God's anger to the cross with Him and "there is therefore now no condemnation for those who are in Christ Jesus" (Rom. 8:1).

Prophetic people also struggle with the church's weakness, indifference, and complacency.

They are aware of the holiness of God as revealed to them by the Holy Spirit, and this informs heavily upon their view of sin in the church.

Depending on their level of maturity in Christ, they will exhibit different levels of impatience with the church's unwillingness to change. A prophetic person who isn't doctrinally well situated regarding their own failures before God will struggle the most with the worldliness they observe in others.

Pastors should review and adjust any harshness in the prophetic person and follow up with them to determine what issues may be causing their irritation. They must model the patience and compassion they wish to see their struggling prophet project to those they call out for sin. In their confrontation, help them see how the Father deals with our sin through the lens of the cross and finished work of Jesus Christ.

Prophets who are hypercritical of the Church are often weak in their understanding and personal application of the gospel in their own lives. They also can struggle with the Father's love for them personally, which is why they cannot seem to extend that love to His Church. "We love, because He first loved us" (1 John 4:19).

While a pastor cannot humble anyone—only God can do that—they can lovingly point them to the place where humility is best grown—the gospel.

Prophetic people have strong emotional ties to what they receive and can be prone to emotional outbursts in the delivery of a message. Work with them on developing the fruit of self-control.

Due to the way the Spirit develops prophetic people, they may be prone to significant emotional moments. This might occur when they are ministering amidst difficult seasons in their personal life. It can also just be a level of immaturity in their prophetic experience.

Sometimes this can produce significant tears or sobbing, getting choked up while sharing, voice quivering, increased volume, intense spasms, and/or bodily movement. A strong emotional response can be the body's natural way of releasing an intense flow of the Spirit, but it can also be unsettling to observe.

Prophetic people should feel free to respond to the Holy Spirit's emotional stirring in times of personal worship and prayer. However, in public service of ministry, counsel them to manage their emotions to prevent distracting the recipients of the Holy Spirit's message. ("The spirits of the prophets are subject to prophets"—1 Cor. 14:32).

The Spirit does not require emotion to communicate His messages or impart anointing. The overwhelming nature of prophetic unction must be trained to serve the saints, not the prophetic individual. Heavy emotions shared in a prophetic delivery can be awkward, distracting, and self-serving. The emotional outburst could be communicating that the recipient may be missing out in some way.

While it may seem real enough and anointed to the prophetic person, everyone else is hoping they will get through what they have to say before they really "lose it."

Pastors need to train their prophetic members to embrace self-control, to avoid significant emotional delivery, and to serve with compassion and clarity.

...their attitude toward the leadership team and members of the local church...

Prophetic people need to feel important and that their contribution matters to their leadership team. Create contexts for them to share their heart and concerns.

Prophetic individuals need a lot of what their ministry is designed to be for others: encouragement, edification, and comfort.

They may appear hardened and tough on the exterior, often giving the impression of impregnable self-sufficiency, but that is largely insecurity in whom they are and where they fit in the body of Christ.

Prophetic people are never fully secure with where they fit in the local Body of Christ. Leaders could affirm them a hundred times in a particular way, but it may still require a hundred more to make it stick. Feeling like an outsider looking in is natural, because that is exactly what they do each week. They are taking a broad view of the church, as God reveals what He wants to say to them.

Depending on how they believe they were heard by the members, which is usually not measurable, the prophetic person may draw negative conclusions. They may isolate themselves, little by little, not knowing how they came across. A lack of direct feedback tempts them to believe they offer less value than they actually do.

One way pastors can help the prophetic person sense their value, even if they don't agree with everything they say, is giving them undistracted time to speak their mind. Benefiting from someone listening isn't unique to prophetic ministry; it's true in every context of authority, but I can personally attest to the faith-building encouragement I've received when my leaders have been willing to hear me out on topics they may, or may not, agree on.

Prophetic people can draw attention to themselves or have a high view of their position, without meaning to do so. Be the friend they need to keep them in touch with reality.

Prophetic people are bold and convincing under the anointing of ministry. It's important to discern the shared content to determine what motives may be present. It's also important to gently confront ambition where it is obvious, drawing more attention to God's faithfulness than their failure.

Confidence in delivery can be misread and off-putting; therefore pastors should be that much more vigilant to identify it, graciously correct it as needed, and then unswervingly trust the Holy Spirit to break the self-promoting tendencies being shown.

Like the swagger of a young athlete, pastors should work on the swagger (arrogant delivery) but not diminish the athletic talent (prophetic risk-taking and highly productive value of what prophetic people do at their best). Build a friendship with the person to understand where there are openings to address anything that is inappropriate.

This is a process that will continue over years, so there is no one confrontation or moment that will set the prophetic person "right." Only God's love and kindness can truly break young stallions properly and make them fit for the Master's use in a race.

Another aspect of confidence bleeding over to arrogance is believing they are shielded from a pastor's correction, because if God had an issue, He'd speak to them directly...except God is interested in building our humility; so be gentle in correcting this incorrect assumption.

Also correct the faulty belief that hearing God means He favors the hearer. While it's true that prophetic persons are blessed and highly favored, they are not more important to God than others. Pastors must find a way to establish a prophetic person's confidence in God that isn't driven by this presumptuous idea.

While pastors are observing this discipleship process play out by the Holy Spirit in a prophetic person, address what needs addressing and be ready to work them through some substantial seasons of breaking that comes by the Holy Spirit. If they are anointed and being used of God in their sin, be assured God intends to make them infinitely more fruitful by pruning them to bear more fruit.

Pastors are not usually the primary agents of this pruning; rather they are the tangible agents of God's love, compassion, and forgiveness toward pride and failure, ensuring the prophetic person doesn't quit his or her faith. The deep dealings of the Holy Spirit are substantial and will require the pastor's full measure of grace and expressed faith in friendship with his prophetic people to keep them moving forward toward God and their calling.

...their personality/character/leadership style within the church...

Prophetic people tend to have a very sensitive conscience, which they can turn on themselves. Turn their attention outward and upward.

Monitor your prophetically gifted for self-condemnation and self-pity, because they will turn their gift inward on themselves when convicted of sin and failure.

Prophetic people can become their own worst enemy by not holding fast to the truths of the gospel in their lives. They are very aware of their ongoing issues of sin and are prone to self-disqualification from ministry.

Prophetic people will also tend to step back when repositioned or corrected for failure in their prophetic ministry. If they make a mistake, or "miss it," they are tempted to pull back. Ideally, no one wants to hurt anyone, but they can easily miss issues in their lives that are impacting their ministry's effectiveness.

Rather than embracing the powerful grace and forgiveness of the cross, they may step back from prophetic ministry, not feeling worthy or prepared to be used. They listen to the lies of the enemy suggesting they aren't really gifted and become content to let others do the ministry. This performance mentality is legalism wrapped in false humility.

Pastors with great compassion and discernment are uniquely qualified to lead them out of these self-defeating mindsets. It helps to get them thinking outside themselves with serving opportunities and upward toward God with prayer times. It also helps to get them sensing their value in the pastor's encouragement of their gift and its potential.

Prophetic people are very bold in their ministry but can be very weak in other aspects of their character. Be prepared for immaturity in the gift.

The dichotomy of bold, genuine prophetic ministry and failed personal character can be very challenging for leaders observing these massive swings between the Spirit's gifting and their everyday life. Like Elijah, they can be taking on the prophets of Baal in one moment, and hiding in an emotional cave of self-pity in the next.

Their capacity to hear God speaking and share that with others so boldly falsely gives the impression that they are applying what they are hearing to their own lives.

Leaders looking to shepherd prophetic people must expect that not only will the prophetic person not always be applying what they are saying to others, but they can appear completely oblivious to the need for these important truths to be applied to themselves.

The more gifted yet immature they are, the more prone to missing the character issues they will be. This doesn't mean the pastor is responsible for addressing all character flaws to keep them humble, but rather to be sensitive to what the Spirit seems to be addressing in each situation and pursue only that.

The pastor may be tempted to pile on the correction in response to the prophet's audacity, but restraint is recommended to spare the prophetic person sorrow upon sorrow.

Pastors need to discern where the Spirit is walking gently and follow Him through to the prophetic person's restoration.

Because some prophetic people can be immature, this can lead to significant mood swings in their everyday lives. They should be encouraged in the doctrines of Scripture and the gospel to stabilize their experience.

Prophetic people not only need to control their emotions in ministry, but also in their day-to-day lives. Because they are prone to substantial mood swings, they must be vigilant to study the doctrines of Scripture and the gospel as buoys they can grab before drowning in the ocean of emotion.

The key is for the prophetic person to accept what is happening as the ongoing ministry of the Holy Spirit and be good stewards of their emotions as they pursue self-control in the service of others.

Drawing attention to one's significant burden for the Church, regardless of its magnitude, and the resulting emotions, only leads to self-service and promotion.

Prophetic people must learn that these kinds of emotional responses are normal and will pass, by the grace of God that is working mightily in them.

Pastors can help them work through their struggles by easily identifying with them through their own significant burden for the Church and sharing how they daily apply the truths and doctrines of grace and the gospel to stay balanced and emotionally solvent.

...their attitude toward relationships with others in the church

Prophetic people are often comfortable spending a great deal of time alone. They need to be encouraged to pursue relationships.

Prophetic people can tend toward the periphery in social circles. This doesn't mean they mind people being around and they do enjoy relationships, but they are often content when they are by themselves with God.

Prophetic people have a unique ability to unplug from the world around them. This includes stepping back from relationships in any context that distracts them from their desire to pursue the Holy Spirit in the prophetic. This may give people the wrong impression that they aren't being friendly or approachable.

They will gravitate toward relationships with other prophetic persons around them. It's their common burden that draws them together. It's important that prophetic people have vibrant relationships with many different people in the church, lest they become so focused on the prophetic that they lose touch with every day realities of life. They need to sustain connection with family, friends, and work to keep them from drifting into a hyper-spiritualism that is self-absorbed and lacks the capacity to build up the church.

Pastors can help the prophetic person find a workable balance between their desire for isolation and the importance of developing meaningful relationships within the church.

Prophetic persons may care more about truth and integrity than people. Challenge their need to be right while highlighting the love of Father for His church.

It's not easy for prophetic people to surrender a point they feel is true. At times, they may fight for the position they feel is right, while missing the need to consider the position of others. This typically stems from a prophetic person's insatiable love of being right instead of people.

This can surface in a substantial way when they are relating to their pastors on unresolved issues in the church.

The burden to make their point heard and acted upon overwhelms their sense of compassion and consideration of others. This is an immaturity of character that pastors need to patiently help the prophetic person discover through questions that reveal the overbearing nature of their attitude.

Pastors can help them see the need to love the people of God more than being right. By reminding them of the value of the sovereign faithfulness of God to His church, pastors can show them how to rest in the Lord and cease from striving in making their points.

Chapter 15

Serving the Messengers

Discipling Prophetic Ministry by Serving the Prophetic People

The following descriptions and encouragements are meant to identify many pastoral attributes and biblical pastoral qualities with regard to prophetic ministry in the Church. Some of these references are inferred from Scripture, and some are just shared from personal experiences serving pastoral ministry in the local church as a prophetic person.

This isn't an exhaustive list, nor will every point apply; consider them suggestions of things to look for in leading prophetic ministry.

What pastors/elders need to prayerfully consider being for their prophetic people...

...in their attitude toward the prophetic gift ministry/delivery to the church...

Pastors have a tendency to view prophetic as a "messy" ministry. Please be patient.

Prophetic ministry can be filled with half-revelations, incomplete interpretations, and flimsy applications. Some pastors may prefer to minimize, or remove altogether, congregational exposure to this kind of short-circuiting ministry. They see preaching and teaching ministry as a sound flow of electricity through a properly conducting and restrained wire to the people of God. It feels dependable, predictable, safe, and controlled.

Unchecked prophetic ministry is "messy" and dangerous, like a loose electrical wire, broken free from its restraint and requiring the people to back away from its arcing and sparking flashes. Though it's exciting to watch where it will flare up next and it can be very powerful, it's just not very practical to serving the local church.

Prophetic ministry really can't be helpful to a church until it's patiently discussed and discipled through mutual, humble submission between leaders and members. Also, it will require post-delivery feedback and accountability for what is being said and how it is delivered.

While pastors aren't the one speaking in prophecy, they are responsible for what a prophetic person says to the Church. Trust God to care for His church more than you do.

Pastors should desire all God wants for the church, but they also understand that whatever they release, they are ultimately responsible for in the body, including any prophetic words. This is why the pastor needs to help the prophetic person(s) understand how and when a prophetic word is delivered.

However, it's also true that the Holy Spirit is very aware of what each church needs, and while He isn't worried about offending them, He can lead the prophetic people into the manner of the delivery as much as He has made known the revelation. Pastors must trust the Spirit while encouraging their prophetic team members to seek God for both the message and the manner in which it's delivered.

He told us exactly who He is and what He is like in Exodus 34:5-7a:

The Lord descended in the cloud and stood with him there, and proclaimed the name of the Lord. The Lord passed before him and proclaimed, "The Lord, the

Lord, a God merciful and gracious, slow to anger, and
abounding in steadfast love and faithfulness, keeping
steadfast love for thousands, forgiving iniquity and
transgression and sin, but who will by no means clear
the guilty."

This is the description of the God who prophesies through
us. While pastors must clearly address error and disorderliness,
they must believe the Spirit loves the church beyond anything
they can comprehend. He desires to give prophetic ministry that
reflects His name, is full of mercy and grace, is slow to anger,
abounds in steadfast love and faithfulness, keeps forgiving
iniquity and sin, and leaves the judgment of the guilty to Him.
He will ensure that every word from Him is saturated with the
truth of the gospel of Jesus Christ and the hope it gives every
person.

*Pastors are under a lot of pressure and responsibility to
serve and mature the church. Delegate.*

"And what you have heard from me in the presence of
many witnesses entrust to faithful men who will be able to teach
others also" (2 Tim. 2:2).

Pastors must care for the flock, have compassion on the
flock, counsel the flock, and if necessary, protect the flock
from harshness or man-centered ministry in the prophetic.
Pastors could very well love the idea of a prophetic ministry
team, and they would love it even more if they had someone to
administrate it biblically and responsibly that they trust won't
lead them astray.

For a pastor who doesn't trust those gifted around him,
this can be tantamount to asking a wolf to tend the sheep. There
must be prayer for maturing prophetic gifts that can work with
leadership in the local church to assist in administration and
development or the hope of "prophetic team ministry" will be
nearly impossible.

To get started, pastors can seek the help from relationships with leadership prophetic people that aren't members of their local church but have proven Ephesians 4 level gifting, are submitted to their local church leadership, and have experience in building prophetic team ministry. These prophetic leaders can provide assistance, impartation, and encouragement in developing prophetic gifts to serve the local church.

I've had the privilege of serving churches in this way, and the practical interaction not only greatly encourages the leadership to move forward, but it also provides their prophetic people a powerful infusion of faith and instruction in how to serve their pastors better.

Pastors genuinely don't know what to do with a lot of what prophetic people bring to them in the name of "hearing" God. Trust God and take the training deeper.

In corporate ministry times, a leadership team may find that some of what prophetic people bring forward is just so non-specific, unrelated, or irrelevant to what they are seeing that it isn't edifying, worth saying a lot about, or giving time to review beyond a first read. This leaves the pastor asking the prophetic people to return to the Lord and seek Him for more, and if there is no more, then to wait on the Holy Spirit for greater clarity. If this happens often, it could discourage both the leaders and those seeking to serve prophetically.

In developing this gift, there will be stops and starts, missed interpretations, and poor applications. This only means leaning deeper into the Spirit for His leading and ministry. The Holy Spirit is sovereign and will not withhold what is needed to serve the Church. Pastors need to challenge their prophetic people to press deeper into His presence, work on improving their prophetic training process, and continue allowing prophecy while waiting on Him for the clarity.

...their service to the prophetic team members of the local church

Pastors should be more concerned with the prophetic

person and their family than with any ministry the prophetic person is building. Help them watch their life and doctrine closely (1 Tim. 4:16).

> Him we proclaim, warning everyone and teaching everyone with all wisdom, that we may present everyone mature in Christ (Col. 1:28).

> And he gave the apostles, the prophets, the evangelists, the shepherds and teachers, to equip the saints for the work of ministry, for building up the body of Christ, until we all attain to the unity of the faith and of the knowledge of the Son of God, to mature manhood, to the measure of the stature of the fullness of Christ (Eph. 4:11-13).

Prophetic people tend to become fixated on ministry to the exclusion of their family's needs and personal growth. Knowing this weakness in prophetic people, pastors may be uneasy about too quickly raising up prophetic ministers.

The power of true prophetic ministry is not how long the gift's been exercised or how accurate, nor frequency of service, but rather how God was glorified in the obedience and humility to serve where and when He calls.

Men may witness to a valid prophetic ministry, but only the Holy Spirit authenticates it by anointing and accuracy. That grace of authenticity is only available to those willing to humble themselves under God's mighty hand, that He may lift them up in due time after they have taken care of their primary obligations in their homes and personal lives. The richest encouragement I know for the prophetic person is in 1 Peter 5:5-9:

> In the same way, you who are younger, submit yourselves to your elders. All of you clothe yourselves with humility toward one another, because, "God opposes the proud, but shows favor to the humble." Humble yourselves, therefore, under God's mighty

hand, that he may lift you up in due time. Cast all your anxiety on him because he cares for you. Be alert and of sober mind. Your enemy the devil prowls around like a roaring lion looking for someone to devour. Resist him, standing firm in the faith, because you know that the family of believers throughout the world is undergoing the same kind of sufferings.

It's all there. Submission to authority, the exhortation to humility, the reason revealed in God's favor, the call to wait on God to raise up the gift, and in the process casting anxiety upon the Lord. There is also the encouragement to remain alert and sober-minded, not drunk in selfish ambition and pride. The enemy is ever seeking to sideline God's prophetic voices; because He knows what a blessing they can be to the church if they find their way to the humility He is calling them to.

Pastors should never care more about the gift than about character growing in his prophetic team. The gift should be a meaningful part of the prophetic life and the church, but never to the exclusion of character. Help the prophetic person keep a clear conscience in their life and doctrine so they can serve wholeheartedly.

The only lasting validation of true gift ministry we have is character. The evidence of a life submitted to Christ, His ongoing conviction, and His sanctification by the Holy Spirit.

Pastors may be open to prophetic growth, but they can tire quickly of having to build the same bridges to the prophetic ministry people over again. Please don't give up.

Pastors may be willing to build bridges of risk-taking acceptance, tentative invitation, and openness emotionally, personally, and ministerially to the prophetic people, only to have them torn down in misunderstanding, misinterpretation, and misapplication of their willingness to be more open. The prophetic people can feel the pastor's marginal enthusiasm to include the prophetic isn't enough, or they take advantage of the pastor's openness as an occasion to push too far.

Some pastors are genuinely trying to make room for prophetic people to share their gift with the body, despite the risks. But, some prophetic people can feel restrained or hindered by the need to submit words ahead of time, the lack of time during worship to share outside of limited windows, and the little to nonexistent, feedback they may receive after they share.

Prophetic people who are untrained in their gift and its administration can often become unmanageable and unreasonable. They think freedom is the ability to do or say whatever they want, the way they want, when actually true freedom in Christ is the exact opposite. However, if the pastors grow weary of revisiting this process with frustrated prophetic people, then they will be tempted to end the process.

Once again, I ask you to remember the grace of God to extend patience and mercy from the gospel. Persevere in serving those who seem unwilling and the Holy Spirit will change their hearts.

Pastors may want the Ephesians 4 demonstration of the gift in the church, but without "team players" it'll be more difficult. It just means they will have to trust, train, and grow them.

Pastors have no way of knowing how this can happen if all they see is prophetically gifted people making demands on their time to hear them, challenging the Sunday service administration, and criticizing preaching ministry with little to show for it in return but a solo act of prophetic ministry that includes semi-specific words, shallow content, and limited anointing.

Why should they risk giving that much opportunity or authority to someone who appears unwilling to invest in the Church?

They will need doctrinal repositioning, reassurance, and a biblical perspective. This will take risk and courage on the part of the leadership, but that resolve will encourage the prophetic members to grow and respond more readily to the Spirit and their authority in the local church.

This is where the better approach of prophetic team ministry will shine. It doesn't highlight any one person, but rather the gospel, grace, and goodness of God. One may rise to an Ephesians 4 level gifting at some point, but they will only care about serving the church and not their selfish ambitions because they started within a team and not on their own.

Pastors are inundated with people who have important causes and ministries to be developed. They must elevate the prophetic because the Holy Spirit did.

Pastors must carefully discern God's will to move the church forward, which includes prioritizing time spent on developing prophetic ministers. Avoid the tendency to default to your own kind, that is, people to care for the people, as opposed to people who tell what the people need to be doing. Pastors will naturally gravitate to those called to their own care ministry. Prophetic people were always together in Scripture for the same reason. There is an ideal reproduction that occurs "after its kind" in creation that is applicable in the church. Pastors train pastors and prophets train prophets.

This doesn't mean pastors can't build a prophet's character; it just means that there will be a limit to what a pastor can do for a very gifted prophetic person. Preferably, it requires a prophetic person to assist the pastor in developing another's prophetic gift as it grows.

However, if pastors don't make the initial step in growing prophetic ministry in the church, then it's less likely to occur on its own. The Holy Spirit commanded this ministry to continue and will raise up prophetic persons to serve and reproduce if the leadership team makes it a priority first.

Pastors should want everyone involved in a ministry context, not as spectators watching just one person doing prophetic ministry.

Prophecy is never about the prophetic person, it's about God's glory revealed in the Church. No one gifted person should always be the focal point of prophetic ministry or the only one God uses to prophesy. This is the importance of team ministry, as the Holy Spirit uses the parts of the church body as He wills to manifest His message and encouragement.

Pastors can help this by encouraging all the members of the church to be seeking the Lord for what He might do through them corporately or individually to edify the church.

Once again, it will also serve the local pastor to connect with proven, experienced, prophetic gifts who share their perspective on development, even extra-locally, to accelerate this process. With today's technological advances, it's more possible than ever to access like-minded resources to reduce developmental prophetic ministry damage.

...their relationships with the prophetic team members in the church

Pastors are not being exposed to the same trials and challenges as prophetic persons. Seek to understand them before taking things they say personally.

God is building endurance in prophetic people, so He will expose them to a volume of trials internally and externally that will require a strong doctrinal foundation to sustain them.

Prophetic persons must have the integrity to admit their anger at God and repent and receive grace for change. They must be willing to hear the pastor's counsel to endure the trials with joy and trust in the Lord.

Pastors will get further in their growth of prophetic ministry development over a cup of coffee and talking than in any teaching or training they offer. Prophetic people need the gifts of wisdom and kindness offered by the pastor to remain strong in their faith.

The pastor must guard against taking things the prophetic person says in frustration personally. God is dealing with them and they are venting where they feel safe. Resist the urge to build barriers.

Pastors are likely to assume that prophetic people have their affirmation in hearing God. Don't overestimate the gift's blessing on the prophetic person.

Pastors see the gift as a blessing they may not have, and they therefore may assume having the gift is encouragement in and of itself. However, prophecy bears its own burden; hearing the voice of the Lord is an awesome responsibility. Pastors will do well to remember how their congregation may not understand the pastor's burden to prepare a message each week.

In fact, because message prep is significantly more time-consuming and difficult, pastors may be prone to unwittingly consider the prophetic burden as infinitesimal because it doesn't require any preparation.

A pastor's actions, lack of response, and lack of feedback may be perceived as indifference by a prophetic person. As a member of a prophetic team for many years, I have seen the prophetic team struggle with this disconnect...and our pastors are models of acceptance!

Because trust is the most important aspect of developing submitted prophetic ministry, avoiding this perception, while it should be two-way, is often the responsibility of the pastor (though one would hope the mature members of the prophetic team would pitch in). Pastors will best be served maintaining regular and open dialogue with their prophetic people, drawing out these perceptions, and seeking forgiveness and understanding from both parties.

Pastors are painstakingly painting the image of Christ in the church; prophetic people point out the missed spots. Embrace a long-term view of the prophetic maturation process.

Through the palette of grace and gifts they have been given, as they best understand it, pastors are painting Christ in the church, and they have no patience for a person who figuratively wanders in and starts criticizing the paint, the brushes, and the artist's manner of ministry to do it.

This could be used to undermine the work of the pastor as well as the faith he must have to walk out his calling in that context. That Hey-buddy-you-missed-a-spot-in-your-painting-up-there mindset coming from the prophetic person is not only irritating, but also discouraging to the pastor. The pastor may feel prophetic people neither understand nor appreciate the sacrifices they make on a daily basis.

Prophetic persons are primarily called to encourage, edify, strengthen, and comfort with their ministry in the New Testament, not criticize, nitpick, and find fault.

People, including pastors, are motivated by encouragement that makes them feel valuable and important in doing God's work for His glory in the Church. This doesn't mean there can never be criticism, but true prophetic correction fills the hearer with hope and faith for what God can and will do with them. The prophetic person must learn to see the local church as God sees them and then prophesy that to the people. Prophetic people are to be heralds of hope, not harassment.

Pastors will need to overlook offenses and unfiltered comments made by prophetic people who don't understand nor appreciate their sacrifices on a daily basis. Prophetic people struggle with balancing compassion and correction irrespective of position or title. Pastors who see this stark harshness as immaturity and not willful insubordination will be able to remain emotionally stable enough to respond with the patience necessary to build trust. This perspective will also help the pastor to remain open to times when the prophetic person's words faithfully bring the Spirit's conviction.

Pastors often don't feel they can correct without deeply hurting the prophetic person's feelings. Keep in mind that "faithful are the wounds of a friend" (Prov. 27:6 KJV).

This is something they don't particularly want to do, so as not to harm or crush a church member. It can be intimidating to face someone who thinks they hear God. Pastors aren't always clear on the validity of a word either, so it can make it doubly difficult for them if the prophetic person is not teachable in their manner or spirit.

This is on the prophetic person to present an approachable, responsive spirit with regard to input and correction. This is the sign of a person in whom the fruit of the spirit is evident. For a pastor, the prophetic person's most convincing attribute is not accuracy of content; it's humility of character. Yet when it's absent, the pastor must come alongside as coach and encourager. They must also remember that at times inflicting a corrective wound now, as a faithful friend will produce last fruit to the glory of God.

Chapter 16

Prophetic Discipleship Done Decently and In Order

"...Decently and in order." (1 Cor. 14:40)

Just as the elder team's example of team ministry should be the backdrop for what is expected of the prophetic team ministry, a similar application can be made in how the pastor disciples the prophetic ministry team. It should be done "decently and in order."

Decently

The word *decently* invokes kindness, sweetness, and social intelligence. It speaks of "conforming to a recognized standard [Scripture] of propriety, good taste, modesty in behavior or speech" (Google Dictionary).

This approach will be the foundation of the pastors' credibility in the prophetic development process. If they are in any way fearful, faithless, impatient, ungrateful, or inconvenienced in the process, it will undermine the willingness of the prophetic members to humbly submit to the local church's authority in leading it. To expect decency from the prophetic people in the ministry but not reciprocate with ministry inclusion, expressed faith, and pursuit of growth can hint at hypocrisy that they will be tempted to resent.

Practically speaking, it just means that the elder team must keep its promise to grow the team and its opportunity. There is much for the elder team to do in caring for the local church's needs, but that isn't what the prophetic person thinks about when they are told that the ministry will be given contexts, focus, and opportunity, and yet it never materializes.

To not be given the chance to grow and experience God's grace in the gift of prophecy because the elder team is reticent, controlling, or unwilling is disheartening and inconsistent with their clearly stated role in Scripture. "Decent" discipleship in terms of a prophetic team ministry initiative should be intentional, faith-filled, and enthusiastic. It should include each of the following steps our Lord Jesus took in building His team.

1.   Recruiting the willing, broken down, and discouraged

Jesus called fishermen, tax collectors, and average men (Luke 5:1-11)

Jesus didn't pursue the learned and religious when He put together His team; He called the average. He didn't need their abilities and talent; He wanted their hearts. He knew if He had their hearts, the Holy Spirit would take care of the rest. He won their hearts' trust to leave everything and follow Him through *encouraging them* ("Depart from me; for I am a sinful man"—Peter in v. 8; "Do not be afraid"—Jesus in v. 10), *serving them* ("were astonished at the catch of fish that had been taken"—the disciples in v. 9), and *envisioning them* ("From now on you will be catching men"—Jesus in v. 9).

This would also involve the pastors seeking out those hurt or offended by past breakdowns in ministry development or opportunity. It would include drawing out their dreams, listening to their needs, and slowly rebuilding the trust that once fueled their passion.

This is best done through Jesus' example with understanding, forgiveness, and the application of the gospel to the situations that have sidelined their interest in the purpose of God. Once addressed, we need to pray the Holy Spirit renews their love for His Church and His purpose.

2.   *Relating to the team members individually and as a group*

Jesus taught His disciples privately and shared a life with them (Matt. 24:3)

This next step would include the creation of fellowship opportunities that become the soil for genuine personal relationship through Scripture study, ministry mentoring, and shared experience. In the midst of this season of discipleship of the team members, pastors want to be identifying, encouraging, and developing the grace gifts of God resident in them.

This was a powerful step taken by our senior pastor, Aron Osborne, that caused the work of the Spirit to explode forth from our team after a long season of dryness due to busyness and the cares of life. He listened to what mattered to us, saw where God was working, and then provided legitimate ministry opportunities for the whole team to move forward in a way that was life changing.

3.   *Raising up by faith*

Jesus sends out the seventy-two (Luke 10:1-12)

Jesus didn't just show His disciples how ministry was done; He created a context for them to be raised up and sent out to experience it for themselves.

The next step is to elevate the entire team's view of Jesus the Savior, their understanding of the gospel, their use of the gifts they've been given, and their access to ministry contexts for their sphere of gifting.

This can be done by generating an equipping atmosphere of identifying gifts and callings, providing workshops, and ministry exercises while keeping an emphasis on accountability, authenticity, and credibility. In this season, we want to continually leverage prophecy in our discipleship process as a way of discerning calling and sphere-of-ministry levels in the team members.

4.   *Releasing for the glory of God*

Jesus gives the Great Commission and promises His Holy Spirit to begin His work (Matt. 28:18-20; Acts 1:5)

Jesus not only came to give His life as a ransom for many, but also to prepare a team to fulfill His purpose in the earth. The cycle of discipleship continues through the faith-filled release of those called, to go forth and recruit, relate, raise, and release others through their ministry.

By commissioning the prophet, challenging bigger steps of faith in the team, and inviting the church corporately to explore all the gifts of God's grace, the elder team is demonstrating their across-the-board commitment to their own Ephesians 4 ministry call to equip and build up the church.

In creating ministry contexts consistent with their sphere of gift, providing needed feedback, and cultivating greater obedience through encouragement and exhortation, they are "conforming to the recognized (biblical) standard," or being "decent," in their commitment to the prophetic ministry. All that remains is to provide the order to perpetuate the process of God's grace manifesting in the church.

In Order

Jesus was not only committed to the broad process of discipleship in recruiting, relating, raising, and releasing His charges, He was careful to follow the Father's direction in how everything should be done.

There was an order to Jesus' ministry that is always evident in the chaos around him. It was always strategic and purposeful. From who the Father healed through Jesus and why (that the works of God could be seen in Him — John 9:3), to the woman who pressed through the crowd and touched Him (Luke 8:45), to the wind and waves obeying His command, and to Pilate turning Him over to be crucified (John 19:11), He was always in control.

God is a God of peace and assurance because everything is under His control, not because everything always goes as we expect. He is sovereign over every man's sin and sanctification.

This means He has a plan that cannot be thwarted. There is an order He will bring out of that which seems strange in the prophetic ministry. He will never let any man take the credit for what He weaves together by His grace, and that may include allowing things to happen that make no sense, or require dependence upon Him. The elder team will need to obey the Father, apply the truth of Scripture, and trust Him for the outcome. Here again we use Jesus' approach to team development with the disciples as the model.

1.   Teaming members together

Jesus sent the disciples out two by two to minister (Luke 10:1-2)

Jesus knew who to put together for the purpose He was working toward. The Holy Spirit did the same in Acts 13:1-3 when He put Barnabas and Paul together. Even though they split up later, His purpose was not stopped. He is always teaming people together in the church to build different aspects of their character. He may rework those teams over time, but there is always a strategy in whom He brings together.

When I met Lewis Seifert, I wouldn't have told you we would have ended up working together. He was a financial expert; I was a football coach. He was corporate and wiser; I was physical education and foolish. But when the father says something is good, it makes no difference what we do—He connects who we are as believers in Christ, together.

How did we know we were supposed to work together prophetically?

One evening I was invited to prophesy at one of our local church's small group meetings in a home and he came to audit the meeting. We had talked about my prophetic gift, but he wanted to see it in action. I was sharing the details of a picture I had with one particular person about a trail in the woods with small fires rimming a clearing they approached. After sharing this and a number of other words, Lewis quietly walked up and casually said, "I saw everything you saw, before you saw it, all night. That's something new that's never happened." To meet my dear friend Lewis, you would most appreciate his humility, but his penchant for casual statements about big things God does is an endearing quality. He recounted how the Spirit had shown him we were meant to minister together, and He would confirm it that night. That was nearly twenty-five years ago, and while God has added incredibly gifted people to our team, we are still sharing with, stirring up, and serving wholeheartedly His local church together. God will knit His team together; we need only open our hearts as leaders to the ministry and encourage the process.

The elder team should pay attention to the relationships within the prophetic team that God seems to be growing and bringing fruit from. While it may only be for a season, the Spirit may be doing a specific work in each member through that relationship necessary for something later. The pastors should seek to team people together as the Spirit prompts them for His glory.

2.   *Training members in their use of their gifts*

Jesus rebuked Peter for his lack of faith on the water **(Matt. 14:31)**

Jesus rebuked them for not being able to cast out the demon **(Matt. 17:14-20)**

Jesus was personally involved in giving feedback to the disciples when their faith failed them. He rebuked their lack of faith in doubting He could come through for them.

There will be seasons when the elder team needs to work the prophetic people through their unbelief and weakness in the gifts. They will not be skilled prophetically upon arrival. If they are, someone else had the privilege of walking them through their failures somewhere else. Even the disciples had to be trained in the use of gifts and faith. They had to be walked through their failure, encouraged, and positioned to try it again.

Debi is another long-time member of our prophetic team. As Lewis is a brother to me, Debi is a wonderful sister to me in this ministry. We have been friends for more than twenty-five years in the prophetic, but Debi's start was slow. Her background was heavily conservative and largely cessationist in experience. She was a voracious writer, always filling journals with what she believed God showed her in quiet time. At the beginning, she believed it best to keep all her diary-like thoughts from God to herself. Our leadership team began doing prophetic training classes, which put her in a room with Lewis and me on a regular basis. As our friendships grew from those meetings, our faith for her grew her confidence and she started sharing some of what she was getting from the Lord. She didn't understand what she was getting, but we knew it was clearly prophetic.

It soon became clear to everyone that she had an amazing prophetic gift. She earned the nickname "kodachrome" for the incredible pictures and interpretations God would give her to bless the church. In time, through encouragement and building faith, she grew less dependent on having to write everything down beforehand. Today, she prophesies consistently to our church and others, sees incredibly edifying visions, speaks courageous words of knowledge, equips others in the ministry, and from time to time still shares powerful words from that tattered journal. God used prophetic relationships, cultivated through contexts provided by leadership, to bring forth a mighty gift to the church from a woman who started with no awareness of her gift or how to use it.

The elder team must not be discouraged by the weakness of the gifts they may see at the start; the Holy Spirit is faithful to strengthen His ministry in His servants. I would encourage leaders everywhere to draw strength from Jesus' example of faith in the Father to build His rag-tag team of "unlearned" men into world-changers.

3. *Targeting potential leaders and building into them*

He prayed and sought the Father for the twelve men He was to pick (Luke 6:12-13)

Jesus took the whole night to pray about whom He was

supposed to pick for His team. This time invested points to the importance of His total dependence upon the Father.

Although Jesus knew what was in men's hearts, even He submitted Himself to follow the Father's order of team selection. Jesus knew by revelation what would befall Him, but only the Father knew who would be His team. This wasn't a small series of choices. These men Jesus would pick now have thrones alongside His in heaven.

Throughout the many years we waited to see God release our prophetic ministry, we were very active serving the local church. It can sound as if the leadership was ignorant of our desire to be used, but nothing could be further from the truth. We visited other churches periodically with the pastors, served in small group and church settings all the time, but the timing wasn't right to raise leaders and recognize a team. While we were being used mightily, we just weren't ready. *I* wasn't ready to lead.

My character still needed significant work; love for the Father's church, career timing, and family had to come before it made sense. The leadership made serious efforts to move the ministry forward. About halfway through the waiting season, they invited a proven prophet to come assist us in better understanding how to serve the team, me as a possible leader, and this ministry. I remember the meeting where my pastor told me they had brought the prophet in to learn more about what to do with me and the gift as a time of encouragement validation. I knew it was time to step into my role and lead, but alas, God knew the timing wasn't then. He had graciously sent the prophet to prepare and encourage my heart for the deep work He would have to do to get me ready. While I expected a glorious go-ahead in those days, instead I received a sober prophecy and a promise.

The leadership team had faithfully identified and targeted the potential leader, but the leader wasn't yet ready. God still had to prepare my heart. The prophet spoke about all the wonderful things God would do with me in this ministry, but before that would happen he said, "The Lord will bury your feet in concrete and the winds of adversity will blow on your life until you feel your ankles will break." He promised that in His time, God would make sense of it all, chip my feet from the concrete, remember His promise, and release His grace. I had no idea what that meant. There was a work that only He could do in my heart to prepare me. The leaders had provided the prophetic connection, the soil of faith and relationships, and the teaching of sound doctrine, but only God could grow the prophet.

In your church, the elder team must seek the prophets to lead the prophetic team ministry for God's glory. They must not be swayed by outward appearances, as Samuel was at first with Jesse's eldest son, but they should be asking God to reveal the humble Davids after His heart. David wasn't chosen for the prospect of an error-free future; he actually failed miserably. God looked on His heart. It's because David failed so badly that we must only seek God's choices so that we can trust Him to redeem anything that happens in our future. He will prepare them like David, by teaching them to draw near to Him in worship, to care for His sheep as a faithful shepherd in the church, and He will teach them to kill their lion and bear. He will get them ready to face their Goliaths of selfish ambition, pride, and the fear of man. He will do the preparation, but the leaders must be faithful, like Samuel was, to anoint the right brother, no matter where they might find him in his life.

This is why the pastors must extensively use prophetic ministry to help *build* prophetic ministry. God will reveal His selections through prophetic ministry and impart the gifts needed for His calling on them (1 Tim 4:14; Acts 13:1-3). The prophetic team ministry will grow at the level of faith the elder team has to seek God for His sovereign targeting of those He has called for His purpose. As they respond to His leading and invest in them with faith, He will raise them up in due season.

4.   *Timing the process as the Spirit leads*

Jesus only did what He saw the Father doing (John 5:19)
Holy Spirit said, "Set apart for me..." (Acts 13-1-3)

Jesus prayed to see what the Father was doing and would

do through Him. This wisdom He sought included the manner of His healing ministry and how it would be done. Whether with spit-drenched mud on the eyes or a distant word spoken to a faith-filled centurion, He sought the order of the Father for His ministry in all things.

The Books of Acts should rightly be called the "Acts of the Holy Spirit," because the apostles were simply following His orders and timing in everything.

This is the necessary process of valuing God's sovereignty in the prophetic process. He sees the end from the beginning and knows the right moment to do all things. I was targeted as a leader, but the timing wasn't right. It would be eighteen years before the chisel was laid to the concrete around my feet, and I can tell you without reservation that the warning of the prophet came true. The adversity I faced had many people shaking their heads at the "bad luck" I experienced in business, life, and opportunity. I experienced self-pity and depression on levels I couldn't overcome without Him.

It wasn't until I hit bottom that I realized that I was being delivered from my addiction to the praise and approval of men. I was being humbled and repositioned to value His promise, not the world and its promise. That humbling process is still underway, but without being set free from the burden of my addictions and idols, I would have made a mockery of His work. The absolute treason of my heart in wanting to rob God of glory that was only due to Him had to be exposed for the cross of Jesus Christ to win its full victory in my life. While I still walk every day with a Jacob-like limp after wrestling with God during the long night of waiting, He meets me every morning with hope and new mercy. It took time. His time.

The elder team must be dialed into God's timing for the prophetic ministry, both in discipling them and in releasing them. There can be a temptation to sense they are never "ready" because of the incremental nature of discipleship. Like a parent struggles to let go of a child reaching maturity, the pastors must be prepared to respond to the Holy Spirit saying, "Set apart for me..." in regard to their prophetic team members.

There should be an increasing expectation of God accelerating His release of ministry to His people, as He matures His prophetic team members. This doesn't mean they are leaving to go anywhere, it just means they are commissioned to do what God has called them to do in the local church.

The Spirit's timing to move the prophetic team from permission to commission is entirely His, but the elder team should be operating in faith for that day to come sooner than later. They demonstrate that confidence through an orderly *teaming, training, and targeting* of the Father's choices in preparation for His *timing* to commission them for His glory.

Chapter 17

The Pastor's Discipleship "Toolbox"

Discipleship as Jesus did it serves as an overview of the team-building process. Now, let's look at more specific means of grace the Spirit can give the pastor for training up prophetic people.

It's a toolbox because there is no one right way to disciple someone; it requires multiple applications of grace. Also, anyone who's ever done a difficult job will tell you there is no substitute for having the proper tool to complete the task.

These tools represent the wisdom God provides a pastor in working with prophetic people in their local church. There are many different approaches the pastor can use, depending on the maturity, personality, and sphere of gifting in the prophetic people they serve.

These concepts, while chronologically organized and alliterated for recall purposes, mirror my experience over the past thirty years in my local church with my leadership team.

The Tools

1)   *Confidence: affirming God's desire, through expressed faith, to bless and raise up prophetic ministry and team(s) within the church.*

When our pastors express faith directly to the members of the prophetic team for God to use them in their gifts on a particular "ministry heavy" Sunday, or for a special meeting, there is usually a significant anointing manifested. The pastor may send an email to the team or call each one, but the more specific the pastor is about what they are sensing God will do only increases expectation and faith for God to move mightily among the team. This expressed confidence in God and the team members serves to elevate everyone's focus to Christ and how He wishes to bless His Church.

I don't recall a moment in prophetic ministry that this "pastoral initiation" didn't produce incredible fruit. Since the God-ordained authority of the local church is the pastor-elder, the prophetic team often senses they are receiving the Spirit's enthusiastic preordained response to the leadership's expressed faith for the church.

This is neither a performance nor a "pastor-pleasing" mentality that drives the prophetic person's response. It's completely fueled by their confidence that the Holy Spirit will respond to the faith of the God-ordained authority of the church for ministry to His people. This is also not about continually cheerleading the members into action. It's a Spirit-led prompting that raises the level of expectancy and faith, as His heart for the church is being revealed to the prophetic people.

Faith must permeate every aspect of the elder team's prophetic ministry in the *Direction, Distinction, Discernment, Discipleship, and Development* process.

The root construct of the word *confidence* is *con + fidere*, which means "with belief." According to the Google Dictionary, confidence means, "the state of feeling certain about the truth of something."

The steps taken by the elder team to include this ministry in the life of the church must be intentional, led by the Holy Spirit, and communicated with boldness to the people being asked to participate.

Everything related to the gifts begins with faith, and expressed faith builds faith. There is nothing more encouraging to a prophetic person than when his pastor expresses faith for his growth in the gift. This can be done through ongoing expressed appreciation for obedience to God, acknowledgment of the effectiveness of their contribution at a meeting, or stirring up the gift before a meeting with a pastoral initiation.

2)   *Clarity: communicating doctrinal protocols, scriptural tests, and timing for prophecy corporately and individually.*

Effective prophetic ministry begins with a clear understanding of the doctrine of the gospel of Jesus Christ. ("For the testimony of Jesus is the spirit of prophecy"—Rev. 19:10). Not only does this give a clear picture of what we base our salvation on, but also it provides a bedrock of confidence for the prophetic people to be used, despite ongoing battles with sin. It also gives clear insight into God's love for us, which should greatly increase the confidence to prophesy in believers.

A sound doctrinal foundation will reduce man-centeredness, legalism, pride, and self-sufficiency in their delivery and content. Prophetic ministry should be built on God-centeredness, love, grace, mercy, and hope.

Pastors can learn a lot about a prophetic person's style of delivery from their core understanding of the gospel. If they are not clear on some of the key foundational tenets of the gospel, it might help to work them through the basics, which are:

> *Sin* (Man's singular and un-fixable problem before God)
> *Judgment* (God's holy, righteous wrath toward man's sin)
> *Mercy* (God's preferred expression over judgment toward man's failure)
> *Propitiation* (Christ's required substitutionary sacrifice for man's sin)
> *Justification* (Christ suffering God's wrath for all our sin, leaving us faultless before God)
> *Reconciliation* (Christ's restoration of broken fellowship with the Father)
> *Resurrection* (Christ's eternal victory over sin, death, hell, and the grave)

Love (God's continual expression of kindness and
compassion toward His redeemed children)
Grace (God's unmerited favor and power to transform us
to His Son's image)

Next, visit their understanding of sanctification and how
God's Spirit works in an ongoing way in people's lives to mature
them into the image of Jesus Christ. Talk with them about
their knowledge of the person and work of the Holy Spirit. It
is important to dissect their understanding of the Holy Spirit,
His work in the Church, His objectives on the earth, and His
manifestations of the gifts.

As doctrinal pillars were being reviewed with my leadership
team, there was also a detailed discussion with the prophetic
team members about testing prophecies, timing within corporate
gatherings, and protocols for different types of more in-depth
prophetic utterance. The discussion included an encouragement
to submit corporate words during services beforehand. If we
received highly directive, predictive, or corrective words or any
related to marriage, mortality, and maternity, we would submit
them.

This isn't to say words about these topics are never given,
but only that we should include pastoral care and counsel in the
timing and wisdom of delivery. Foreknowledge of any of these
things requires maturity and discipline in the prophetic person to
properly handle them—with the elder team involved.

If a church employing open congregational sharing has
a prophetic person sharing a message to the leaders because it
touches on sensitive issues, the responsibility for the message
transfers to the local elders to judge whether the word is to be
shared or held back. The prophesying member has, nonetheless,
been obedient to the Holy Spirit in submission. The elder team
needs to communicate clearly with the prophetic team about
how they will handle messages they review and why.

It is wise to also review the protocols regarding the elder
team and the absence of the senior pastor when prophetic
ministry comes to the gathered church. Our pastors traveled

to other churches regularly to preach, so we needed those who remained to identify which elder was overseeing prophetic ministry during the service. It's very important that the prophetic team know whom they can speak to regarding messages and their delivery in the absence of different leaders. It should not always be the case that they must wait for the senior pastor to return, but those remaining elders should be empowered to make the call to serve the church.

3)   Coaching: teaching spiritual disciplines and their value to stabilizing prophetic ministry on the team.

It would seem unthinkable that someone who claims to hear the voice of God can so readily move away from God. But it's that very capacity to hear that can lead to complacency and pride, allowing entry to various kinds of sin. Drift is inevitable in the believer's heart unless it is anchored by the regular application of spiritual disciplines to know Christ better.

In my early years of prophetic ministry, I experienced significant challenges both emotionally and spiritually. I desperately needed the assistance of the entire leadership team to learn and appreciate the value of stabilizing my heart through spiritual disciplines. Due to my highly emotional nature, their consistent investment of sound doctrine through teaching, training, and feedback was critical to being useful.

Pastors committed to discipleship of their members understand the value of spiritual disciplines for the believers' sustained growth toward maturity. The Holy Spirit uses these disciplines to help believers remain steadfast when their flesh and mind are weak and unresponsive to the things of God. Pastors should continually put these before the prophetic people in accountability, as they may tend to rely so much on hearing the voice of God for prophecy that they are prone to drift from the intentional pursuit of their own relationship with Jesus.

There is a horrific warning in Scripture that speaks directly to this issue in those who prophesy:

Not everyone who says to me, 'Lord, Lord,' will enter the kingdom of heaven, but the one who does the will of my Father who is in heaven. On that day many will say to me, 'Lord, Lord, did we not prophesy in your name, and cast out demons in your name, and do many mighty works in your name?' And then will I declare to them, 'I never knew you; depart from me, you workers of lawlessness (Matt. 7:21-23).

Pastors can serve prophetic people well by helping them learn the value of spiritual disciplines that they may not slip into error or think they are further along in their relationship with Christ than they actually are.

Here are a few of the most treasured disciplines that have produced much prophetic fruit in my life and others:

Worship. Authentic praise and meditative worship opens the spirit to receive from God. The power of instrumental worship to stir prophecy is well documented in Scripture (1 Chron. 25:1; 1 Sam. 10:5; 2 Kings 3:15-16).

Study. Scripture study, application, and memorization strengthen the mind against the enemy and the flesh (2 Tim. 2:15; Col. 3:16).

Prayer. Praying and inclining our hearts to God both in mind and spirit to intercede and make requests of Him (Phil 4:6-7; 1 Thess. 5:17).

Fasting. Abstaining from food and preferred indulgences for a period of time to focus on intimacy with God (John 4:34; Matt. 6:16-18).

Reading. Reading God-centered books and articles that increase affection for God and the Church (2 Tim. 2:15; Col. 3:16).

Journaling. Writing down personal experiences and thoughts as well as any prophetic messages or insights (Hab. 2:2-3; Ps. 45:1).

Silence. Turning our mind and spirit's internal chatter to

the least volume and learning to listen for His voice
(Ps. 46:10; Hab. 2:20).

Biblical Fellowship. An intentional pursuit of relationships
for biblical accountability, growth, and maturity (Heb.
10:24-25).

Service. Seeking service to the local church members and
elders in non-visible, practical, and humble ways (1
Thess. 4:11; 1 Pet. 4:11).

Let the word *coach* inspire pastors to train the members
of the team in spiritual disciplines, as they would athletes in
physical disciplines, to improve their capacity to receive from
the Holy Spirit.

*4)   Cultivation. Developing   and   encouraging   team
relationships to build accountability and character.*

Relationships were the key to my personal growth in
the prophetic throughout the years of waiting. These biblical
friendships kept me grounded and focused on serving the church,
not my ministry. We were no less passionate about our being
prophetic; it was just more important that we learned to love
one another and the church more than how we were used. These
lifelong relationships also took the pressure off the pastors to do
all the discipleship as God worked through the team members
to speak freely into my life. I am eternally indebted to these
brothers and sisters for their patience and faith for what God
would do with us.

Prophetic people will naturally be more tempted to things
like pride and independence because of their perceived ability
to hear God speaking to them. This can lead to an unhelpful
isolation that can potentially blind them to what's lacking in
their growth.

In planting a God-glorifying prophetic team ministry that
grows in the local church, pastors should seek character as the
fruit of prophetic maturity, and it should be evidenced in their
active cultivation of relationships as the soil in which it's grown.

Leaders can mistake prophetic authenticity as sensational predictive accuracy, substantial manifestations, and bold declarations. These demonstrations can certainly be of the Spirit's power, but they are no measure of a person's character. Many powerfully graced prophetic ministers have failed to keep their promise to God, the Church, and their families by falling into grievous error and sin.

Meaningful and accountable relationships within the prophetic team—and in the prophetic people's lives personally—will greatly increase the cultivation of character.

Character is the prophetic person's total portfolio of development in all areas, including the fruit of the Spirit, ministry by the Spirit, and submission to the Spirit. Character is the whole package of a prophetic person's current maturity in Christ. Integrity is character's faithfulness, love is character's sincerity, perseverance is character's consistency, boldness is character's confidence in God, and meekness is character's broken disposition.

Character is the pastor's best way to gauge the strength of their prophetic team members individually and as a whole. The best context to measure character in each person is by monitoring the relationships between them and others.

If an individual is unwilling to submit to the loving kindness of God in developing maturity through relationships in the local church, then their credibility is hindered from the beginning. There is no level of accuracy or anointing that can make up for the clanging sounds made by a loveless lone-ranger prophet who becomes increasingly paranoid of other's motives and efforts to help them. The ones who separate themselves from God's people are in danger of being false prophets in the truest sense of the definition.

Character is often said to be what someone is when no one is around. This will always remain the true test of integrity, but in assessing a prophetic person's character, it should be equally observable in the presence of others.

When people are present, leaders can see the priority we as prophetic persons place on other's needs, cares, and desires.

In gatherings, we demonstrate our willingness to serve, submit, and share in relationships. You can listen to our speech and ministry for humility, compassion, and encouragement. In every interaction with others we reveal what we value and whom we deem important. If we are prone to sarcasm, slander, gossip, or uncharitable judgments, this will be obvious when we talk about others. If we are overly talkative or withdrawn in dialogue, we are communicating our own sense of importance or insecurity. I know all these things because it was relationships that brought these sinful patterns to light in me. These are all compelling reasons for leaders to create intentional contexts for prophetic people to interact, practice, and minister.

5)   *Compassion. Demonstrating the Father's heart of love and assurance through expressed encouragement.*

If there is one thing that my leadership excelled in was their ability to express God's compassion toward me and my prophetic ministry. I generated significant collateral damage at times with my pride, misunderstanding of God's mercy, and self-righteousness in prophetic ministry. Being more committed to being right than loving, it was the continual compassion of those God had given me to care for my soul when I began to grasp His love for me. I was repeatedly compassionately reminded by my leadership of their love for me and their patience with the good work God was doing.

This is probably the most important tool a pastor has to develop prophetic ministry. Expressing the love of God to the prophetic person is an extension of the Father's heart for them. This is the single most critical component of discipleship in the prophetic person. They must be deeply anchored in the Father's love for them and His Church. The pastor, who cares for the prophetic person as the Father does, provides a conduit of compassion to flow to their failure, struggles, and trials. The prophetic person will be exposed to ministry from the pastor that models how they will minister prophetically to others.

"Compassion felt for someone" is very much like "gratitude

thought for someone;" it matters little. The only compassion or gratitude that means anything is vocal, intentional, specific, and timely. While compassion is a Spirit-filled awareness of another's need, communicating compassion is a learned skill. Pastors train in this outward expression every day, in counseling, hospital visits, prayer for the sick, and care for the needy. In the prophetic context the most potent form of demonstration is profuse verbal encouragement.

The ability to articulate the importance of, appreciation for, and perseverance in the prophetic ministry members is the key to unlocking the greatest treasures of faith and flow by God's grace in them. If there is ever a moment of wondering what to do for a struggling prophetic person, expressed compassion as verbal encouragement should be the pastor's default.

6)   *Confirmation. Feedback and affirmation are the key to strengthening prophetic ministry.*

Feedback to the prophetic person confirming God speaks through them is a powerful component of sustaining prophetic ministry enthusiasm. The intentional effort of the pastor to seek the prophetic person and offer meaningful insight is of great value. Even if the feedback involves a measure of adjustment, if the message was believed to be from the Lord and encouraging, it is helpful.

The reason it's so important to the prophetic person is that God's ordained authority in the church (the pastor) is acknowledging their ministry contribution. It's critical that the pastors confirm where the Lord was faithful to use them.

There were seasons of trusting God in obedience as my leadership team had grown so accustomed to the prophetic ministry that feedback became increasingly scarce. In fairness, I stopped expecting it, but the absence of communication about the regular prophetic ministry opened a door for the enemy to tempt me into thinking the church stopped valuing my contributions. I was deceptively led to believe they no longer cared whether I prophesied or not. Or worse, that I was an unnecessary interruption to the more valuable ministry of preaching. Still worse, that maybe the church would be safer and better off if I stopped prophesying individually and corporately altogether. After all, would anyone notice or care to say anything? I was in a war with a real enemy who did not want God's people encouraged, period.

We had a microphone set off to the side of the auditorium overseen by an elder for anyone who felt they had something from God to share. I grew weary of stepping out when I was sent back repeatedly and not permitted to share what I thought God was saying. Often the reason for not getting to share had more to do with my pride and irritated attitude than the message. I wasn't coming to serve the church or to love God's people in prophetic ministry; I was bracing for a rejection by an elder at the microphone. My approach was too personal, self-absorbed, and strife-laced to be released, but I just couldn't see it until God did the work necessary to lovingly address it in me.

It was difficult to not feel a measure of shame or self-pity in that long walk back to my seat after taking such a step of faith to go forward to the leaders. This was the Holy Spirit testing my willingness to serve the church and His direction, regardless of how it made me look or feel. I honestly believe my leadership team didn't know what to say to me that would help. However, I still needed the feedback to help me grow. I needed them to help me see any progress I was making in the process, because it was difficult to see it in myself in the midst of the Lord's dealings in my life. Any measure of continued confirmation that I was hearing the Lord, despite my many character issues, no matter how small, was a cup of cold refreshing water in an otherwise dry and weary desert season of frustration and despair at my inability to do things that only trusting God would change.

As with expressed compassion through profuse vocal encouragement, confirmation can be a powerful tool to strengthen the prophetic team and build toward future faith for greater steps to bless the church. I believe some were concerned I might grow increasingly more proud with confirming feedback. This is a lie the enemy used with many friends and leaders to get them to withhold much needed encouragement to help me keep resisting his harsh and repeated attacks on my soul.

It's also important to encourage the prophetic members to challenge one another in giving honest, corrective feedback. Sometimes this "iron sharpens iron" process works best when it comes between two members who respect one another in the prophetic ministry. It's important that the elder team observe the team relationships and encourage the stronger members to review and weigh more critically what is said and how it is delivered.

I've benefited greatly from the honest, direct, unreserved feedback of my prophetic brother Lewis. While it wasn't always easy to hear, I knew he loved me and had my best in mind. It was easier for me to receive the tougher correction from him because I knew he understood the gift and walked in it with me, which somehow made the intensity of the adjustment easier to absorb. If it was always coming from the leadership, I would have easily lost heart with the process, never feeling I measured up to what they believed was necessary.

Over more than twenty-five years, Lewis and I have routinely weighed one another's prophetic contributions with honesty and encouragement. This has led to greater precision, brevity, and clarity in most cases, and it's taught the value of accountability with the gift at all times.

7)   *Correction. Ministry training moments provided through accountability to leadership that are required for greater fruitfulness.*

When it comes to correction, the pastor must patiently seek to build up the prophetic person with the very same things the prophetic ministry should be to others: encouragement, edification, exhortation, comfort, and strengthening.

A direct approach when correction is called for is effective, because prophetic people tend to see things in black and white. This doesn't mean being crass or insensitive, but rather asking direct questions that require answers, producing confession and repentance.

This ability to ask questions that the Holy Spirit used to bring conviction was a common experience with my leadership. There wasn't harshness, just honest queries that revealed significant holes in my theology and a fundamental lack of awareness of others in ministry. They weren't afraid to gently confront my overconfidence and self-righteousness with the grace and patience of the gospel.

I missed so many blind spots in my character because I wrongly assumed that if what I was saying was from God that would guarantee me the same grateful and enthusiastic feedback He was getting. Unfortunately, many loved what God was saying to them but at times struggled deeply with my delivery.

My leadership would faithfully bring the necessary correction to help me better understand what needed to change in my heart toward God's people. There were seasons when I only expected correction due to the frequency of my mistakes. It really never was about what I was hearing, but how I was sharing. This led to another challenge for my leadership in how to correct me without leaving me in self-loathing and self-pity.

Prophetic people can be their own worst enemy without understanding that it's God's kindness that leads to repentance. Although He is never harsh with them, they can mistakenly misapply self-condemning thoughts to God's discipline.

Early on, my shallow personal application of the gospel left craters of condemnation in my heart. I could drop into deep fissures of faithlessness and self-deprecation, making it difficult to help me out of my self-absorption.

We are prone to being like Elijah after a great victory, who, when challenged, ran into a cave of isolation. It's safe to say that most prophetic persons haven't had their lives threatened, but nonetheless, they are prone to run away emotionally, as Elijah did, if they aren't anchored in the gospel.

In these situations, pastors may have to launch a mini-expedition over coffee to locate them in whatever cave they are in and talk them back into prophetic service. As one who has experienced his share of Elijah-like discouragement, I am eternally grateful to my church leadership for not giving up on me.

It's never easy to tell prophetic people they have delivered a wrong message or an inappropriate one. When correction must be done, I would encourage the elder team to be **STRONG** in their efforts to serve the prophetic person:

> *S*pecific. The failure must be shared honestly and clearly. The failure should not be categorical or a total failure.
>
> *T*imely. It must be shared privately as soon as reasonably possible after it was done, and in a one-on-one format.
>
> *R*edemptive. It should be offered with a faith-filled, go-forward strategy that keeps them engaged.
>
> *O*rganized. The correction must be well articulated, concise, and with a purpose.
>
> *N*urturing. The goal should be to build up the person, share with kindness, and listen to their thoughts.
>
> *G*rateful. The process should include ways the leader appreciated their faith, contribution, effort, or risk.

What would we need to "correct" in a congregational prophetic word?

We've covered many potential breakdowns at the end of Part 4 in this book, but here are a few that would be obvious to address:

A)   *Words that are focused solely on correction or harsh calls to repentance that lack redemption and encouragement.*

> If God wants to change a church, He will do it by His Spirit in the hearts of the people through revival, not through a harsh correction from a prophetic voice. As I heard prophet Dr. Ray Self say at Freedom Fellowship in 2014, "We prophesy on the other side of the cross." Jesus took all condemnation and harshness to the cross. I was

susceptible to diminishing the redemptive kindness of God expressed for His church in words I would hear, while emphasizing any warnings or corrections as the priority.

I wrongly believed that if I was being corrected for my struggles, then the church needed it, too.

My resistance to the Father's love in my own heart led to an unwitting harshness in my spirit that was often evident in my delivery until I better understood how to separate God's dealings with me from His delight in His Church.

B)   *Corporate words that are "out of sphere," or that don't edify the present gathered body of believers.*

Sadly, I was enamored with the idea that significant themes in prophecy were synonymous with significant ministry. I had little appreciation for the Father's holy humility in being willing to stoop to the lowest, unseen person to let them know He loved them. To my shame, I expected God to reveal big secrets and words over nations that weren't necessary for a local body to receive.

There are times when we are tempted to embellish or expand our sphere of influence in a message, and we can miss the simple and very generous heart of God to edify His local church. Also, any corporate words that are confusing or lack scriptural accuracy should be adjusted due to their not meeting the biblical mandate of clarity.

C)   *Corporate or Individual words shared that are significantly directive, predictive, or corrective that aren't edifying or cleared with the leadership beforehand.*

The local elder team should receive ahead of

time words that direct, predict, or correct significant elements of the church so they can prepare to pastor the people through the nature of the words. If they let the word go forth, they intend to lead the church through it.

I have received many significantly directive, corrective, and predictive words in my life for others and the church, but have found that part of true submission to local leadership prophetically is my willingness to submit ones that may produce discussion or feedback ahead of time. If I'm not in a position to submit to the leadership team in the moment, I will strongly encourage the person to take what I say to our leaders, or those in their church, for review, prayer, and counsel.

D) *Words focused on man's desires, needs, and wants that don't glorify God nor strengthen the body of believers' awareness of who God is.*

The thrust of true prophecy is edification and building up the Body of Christ. Prophecy is God declaring who He is in our midst, and while it may include man's desires, needs, and wants, the primary focus will be on His desires and will for us.

There is a temptation to seek the approval of men through prophesying the prosperity and fulfillment of what people want. While it's wonderful to deliver good news of what God will do for people, the best news we can deliver anyone is the gospel. The prophetic person can become overly focused on what men will receive from God, rather than drawing the church's attention to God and increasing their affection for God.

8)   *Commitment. Remaining faithful to the prophetic ministry team development process over a long time.*

The seeds planted in any ministry will take time to bear substantial fruit. No one understands the patience required for growth to be evident more than a pastor. They have committed their lives to discipleship of God's Church for His glory. This tool should not be a surprise to them.

However, a commitment to the prophetic ministry is more than seeing individuals grow in their faith and relationship with Jesus Christ. It's seeing the gifts of grace in prophecy released in them, joining them to a team of unique people and working with that team to serve the purpose of God in the local church.

It's hard enough to build an elder team that reflects the glory of God consistently before the church. Building another team with such potential for creating challenges, as prophecy does, could be a daunting task. This is why the elder team's commitment must be anchored in a conviction from Scripture, illumined by the Holy Spirit, that this is a necessary and valuable asset to the kingdom of God.

Our leadership and our prophetic team will admit their struggles over the past twenty-eight years of growing this ministry, but the commitment from both has never wavered. Never has the sentiment "Failure is not an option" been more meaningful to a group of people. Not that we were declaring this or that we didn't fail each other miserably, but this was the promise of God to us. He is faithful to a thousand generations (Deut. 7:9) and with Him in charge of this work, failure was never an option. Our commitment cannot be to building a ministry that is entirely His; we must be committed to obeying Him, and He will bring forth the ministry.

If the pastor or elder team sees the process as not worth the commitment, then the potential prophetic members will either not pursue all God has for them in that local expression, or they will seek outside contexts to minister and be used in their gift, or they will pursue other churches that will work with them. The latter two options may, at first glance, appear acceptable to an elder team not wanting the risk. I would encourage them to prayerfully revisit the Scripture's clear exhortation not to despise prophecy (1 Thess. 5:20) and their mandate in Ephesians

4 to equip and build up the Church.

It can take some time to see God bring a team together that truly honors Him, but it honors Him most when the elder team demonstrates the grace of God on their gifts to commit to serving the prophetic.

9)   *Commissioning. The elder team publicly recognizing the Ephesians 4 prophets and releasing them in ministry to the local church and extra-local Church, as the Spirit dictates.*

When the elder team seeks to use the tool of commissioning a prophet, they should only be publicly affirming the ministry that is already taking place in the local church. Also, there shouldn't be any members in the local church surprised by the leadership team's step to recognize the prophet. This after-the-fact approach is typical for the purposes of proving, testing and evaluating the sphere of a prophet's gift in the local church.

During the prophet's maturation process, the local church will likely benefit greatly from their ongoing ministry, corporately and individually. However, the elders must be patient to allow the Spirit to do the necessary deep-character work of humility and doctrinal preparation. They must not be swayed by the anointing they observe, but only by the Spirit's prompting for the proper time of commissioning ("The Holy Spirit said, 'Set apart for me Barnabas and Saul for the work to which I have called them." — Acts 13:2).

The primary Ephesians 4 role of the prophet is for equipping and building up the local expression of Body of Christ, overseeing the prophetic ministry team in the local church, and prophesying as the Spirit leads. There may be additional extra-local Church ministry included for those whose sphere of gifting warrants it, but their passion should always be to strengthen and equip their local church first.

The prophet's development in the local church will likely play out over an extended period of time, as directed by the Holy Spirit, within the prophetic ministry team and managed by the elders directly involved with them. One reason it took so long for me was because of my significant, and continuing, need for humility and love for the Church.

But, an equally significant reason for the delay in our process was due to the leadership's extremely conservative position on commissioning in general. They didn't believe in titles generally, nor were they very clear on what a prophet would actually do. The revelation has come that while the job description may still need work, it's about the church benefiting from the grace released when the gift is recognized to have a measure of authority. People respond differently to the ministry, training, and exhortation from the leader, and their faith to believe for how God could use them increases. We are still learning the job description, but the grace for growth in the understanding, activation, and function of the gift of prophecy and how it edifies the church has been significant.

There is a significant difference in the prophetic person's influence between the "permission" of the elder team to minister and the "commission" from the elder team to equip the local church as a prophet. Neither is about the importance of the person, but rather the release of the Spirit's anointing in the person for the local church they serve and beyond.

The external recognition by the elder team of the prophet's proven gift and character, coupled with the Spirit's affirmation of the decision, is a powerful combination set loose in the lives of the local, and in many cases extra-local, believers.

Leaders can expect a significant increase in impartation and activation of many other gifts as a result of the prophet being commissioned. The prophet's obedience allows the Spirit to go forth from them to stir up many others in the local church through prophetic words, encouragement, and edification resulting in a multiplying effect of ministry. There will not just be a jump in prophetic ministry, but soon there will be a rise in passion within every ministry of the church, as the prophetic team members continue reaching out, equipping, and building up the church.

The God-honoring result is that the elder team will experience fresh support in the administration of the church because members are being challenged, renewed, and encouraged to take their places in what God has called them to do.

This is a phenomenal fruit-bearing work of the Spirit that must not be rushed, nor presumed upon, lest the prophet fall because they lack the proper maturity to serve and glorify Christ alone. Each elder team should seek the Lord for the prophet to be added to their team, since the impact can be exponentially encouraging to their efforts. The same is true for every other Ephesians 4 ministry that serves the church. It's on the local elders to ask God to supply as only He can.

Governmentally in the local church, the prophet can serve as a vocational elder, which may involve duties particularly designed for the prophetic as well as taking on some pastoral duties in administration of the church. It certainly can be done as the Spirit leads, but as a lay elder (bi-vocational and not drawing his income from the church he serves) they would be less exposed to conflicts of interest in speaking what the Lord is saying to them, free to pursue their service in developing the team and other member's callings, and even helping other churches if they request help. They would not be considered deacons due to the fact that they are Ephesians 4 ministers to the church.

Each elder team must decide how best their gifting fits into their service to the local church, but the commissioned prophet should be recognized as a member of the local church leadership team, even if they aren't recognized as an elder. Also, the local leadership team would be blessed to include the prophet in opportunities to seek the Lord for the church as leaders.

10)   *Connections. Opening doors through elder relationships for extra-local training or ministry opportunities.*

I've spoken about the importance of the elder team creating contexts for the prophetic ministry team in the local church. This tool references another level of pastoral impact on the prophetic ministry: external validation.

I once heard a prominent Bible teacher share that there is an "internal" call in the prophetic person that is validated by the Holy Spirit and His faithfulness to use them. However, the internal call being validated carries little weight until it's validated externally by the pastors who know the minister best in their local church.

This external validation isn't just limited to the commissioning of the prophet, but rather the inclusion of the member in ongoing and increasingly more visible ministry opportunities. This isn't about ambition, or focusing on the person's advancement in the Church, it's about God's affirming favor on His ministry through a redeemed sinner.

The genuine prophetic minister knows there is nothing worthy of honor in him, but to have the Spirit's ministry done through him more often is an unspeakable privilege. This is practically done through the pastor making connections with other pastors and ministries for their prophetic team to grow.

We have seen God open many doors of ministry to our prophetic team within our church and extra-locally through the connection and validation of our local leadership team. It's critical that the leadership team's faith be exercised in positioning those God has called for greater fruitfulness in the Body of Christ. The purpose is not a "branded" ministry for those being used, but a testimony to the grace of God flowing from the local churches to one another through more than just a single person. It's all the saints being prepared and released for the work of ministry in loving one another, the truest demonstration of being Christ's disciples in the earth.

If the elder team invests in the prophetic team to receive training from respected ministries or teams outside the church or sets up ministry to another church or churches with their own local prophetic team(s), it's a powerful statement. The authoritative faith communicated through these extra-local connections raises the bar of accountability and confidence in the local prophetic team from the elders. It's a phenomenally galvanizing step by the leadership to declare God has been faithful to the local church through the prophetic team and they believe it can happen for others through them.

The Goal of Our Discipleship of the Prophetic Ministry Team Members

"...until we all attain to the unity of the faith and of the knowledge of the Son of God, to mature manhood, to the measure of the stature of the fullness of Christ, so that we may no longer be children, tossed to and fro by the waves and carried about by every wind of doctrine, by human cunning, by craftiness in deceitful schemes. Rather, speaking the truth in love, we are to grow up in every way into him who is the head, into Christ, from whom the whole body, joined and held together by every joint with which it is equipped, when each part is working properly, makes the body grow so that it builds itself up in love." (Eph. 4:13-17)

Part 4: The Ministry of Prophecy

Introduction to Part 4

DEVELOPMENT - *How are we going to grow the gift in our local church?*

As we've laid the foundation of where we are going and why, it's important in this final section to frame out various means of grace provided by God to develop prophetic team ministry in the local church. This section will address the protocols, priorities, and types of prophecy that are common in the Church today.

The objective is to connect the dots of doctrine and experience together to form a reasonable path toward a sound, God-honoring pursuit of this ministry to corporately and individually edify our local churches.

186 RECLAIMING PROPHECY / Slack

Chapter 18

Local Church Prophetic Ministry

In the New Testament, Paul highlights the unique nature and value of prophetic ministry to the local church. Paul even elevated prophetic ministry among the gifts God uses for His glory, not to diminish other gifts or preaching, but to encourage us to eagerly desire it. Why?

The answer lies in applying the directives in verses 1 and 39 of First Corinthians to corporate gatherings of the saints.

The Value of Prophetic Ministry in the Corporate Gathering of the Saints

Corporate prophetic utterance for *encouragement, edification, and comfort* is the result of true prophetic ministry according to 1 Cor. 14:3.

But why is prophecy singled out as the gift that edifies? Don't the other gifts edify as well? All the gifts should build up the Church (1 Cor. 12:7), so what is so special about prophecy that Paul felt the need to separate it as something the church should eagerly desire (1 Cor. 14:1, 39)?

What might pastors be missing about prophecy and why does it matter?

Paul addresses people who were speaking out during a corporate gathering of the saints because of confusion over their use of tongues, lack of gift protocol, and talking over one another, among other things. In the midst of all his administration and correction, there is an underlying theme of exhortation to seek to build up the Church (1 Cor. 14:12).

It's in this context that Paul says prophecy is about edification, but that's not the whole picture.

If pastors point to edification alone as the primary objective of prophecy in the local church, they run the risk of encouraging something very God-centric to become something focused on men. This prophetic drift to man-centeredness is caused by continually emphasizing man's needs and desires in the prophetic over God's character and sovereignty in our lives.

The assumption underlying First Corinthians 14:3 on its own is that any words believed to be impressed upon us from God, words that are true and Scripture-worthy and make people feel encouraged, edified, and comforted, would qualify as "prophetic." On the surface, the assumption sounds accurate, but it doesn't explain the fact that many words people share as "prophetic" in a meeting, while often very positive in tone, seem to lack anointing on the message.

Why isn't the same edifying power in every supposed "prophecy" that comes?

What encourages, edifies, and comforts the heart of man most isn't just the acknowledgment and understanding of his need for God. Nor is it the promise of having His needs met by God. Rather it's having God Himself manifest His active presence in our hearts while He's declaring His sovereign control over all things that drives true edification.

"God Is Really Among You!"

The reason for Paul's elevation of prophecy is better captured in chapter 14, verse 25, where he declares that prophecy was a sign for believers that "God is really among you."

He interrupted his administrative diatribe about order, edification, and protocol to drive a doctrinal stake in the ground that should anchor our view of prophetic ministry.

He didn't say edification was prophecy; that's what prophecy *does*. Because prophecy edifies, it prompts the unbeliever's startled reaction to secrets of their heart being laid bare and proclaims, "God is really among you!" This is the sign to believers (1 Cor. 14:22) that true prophetic ministry has occurred. God's manifest presence is undeniably revealed!

True prophetic ministry releases the manifest presence of God, and that is why it matters so much to Paul. It's the Holy Spirit confirming His message with a powerful witness in the hearer's heart that the blessing of His presence is drawing near.

Paul wants us to eagerly desire true prophetic ministry because it's synonymous with an increase in God's manifest presence. And it's that manifestation of Him that truly edifies the Church.

If pastors and their prophetic people are only set on edification as the primary goal, they may find themselves testing a message beforehand only on its potential to edify. This assumes that God will honor any positive, upbeat vocal expression that seems to fit. While there is certainly no sin involved in that approach, there is a sense that something is missing when this becomes the norm.

Certainly "experience" should not trump the truth of Scripture. To claim that God's presence isn't among us if a prophecy falls flat is incorrect, because He is with us, as Scripture promises. But is the local church elder team, its prophetic people, and its members expecting God to manifest His presence among them through prophecy in a manner that richly edifies the believers and startles the unbelievers into exclaiming, "God is really among you!"?

Some pastors may stiffen their spines at this, concerned about emotionalism. It seemed to be Paul's concern, too. So let's look at the difference between experience and emotionalism.

Emotions are inexorably linked to the church's experience of God's presence. How can they not be? God's manifest presence should fire us up and overwhelm us! While Paul encourages us to school our emotions through Scripture, decency and order, it's clear from Paul's example of ecstatic uttering by unbelievers upon hearing prophecy that God engages our emotions intentionally.

Experiencing God's manifest presence through prophecy does involve the pastor's willingness to engage experiential elements of worship and ministry. A balanced integration of doctrine and experience in corporate meetings can be achieved through the fulcrum of the true preaching of the gospel without swinging the pendulum into abject emotionalism or intellectualism.

Surely the unbeliever should not be the only one deeply affected by the manifest presence of God. "God is really among you!" is appropriate for believers, as well. Are we to turn off that response once we become believers? Of course not.

Perhaps the reason Paul stated the believers were merely edified and not startled by God's manifest presence is that they weren't surprised. They expected Him to come and therefore weren't startled but edified.

This expectation of experiencing God in our meetings through prophecy and other means of grace is vital; removing them or downplaying them only serves to remove what makes the church who it is—God's glorious possession on the earth. Dialing back people's responses, affections, and enthusiasm for God is counterintuitive to how God made them. Corinth was overly emotional, but that wasn't Paul's concern. It was directing all that emotion toward an expectation of God's manifest presence through prophecy, not in seeking to elevate man-centered expressions of power and wisdom.

This is why prophecy has been raised as the gift to be sought after by all believers. There's no other gift mentioned in Scripture that carries this unique connection to the manifest presence of God. What teaching is to elevating our doctrine of God in glorifying Him, prophecy is to elevating our experience of God in doing the same.

We don't want prophecy to replace preaching, or emotions to displace authenticity in our meetings; we want prophecy that raises our experience of God to the level of our knowledge about Him.

This is why we often find ourselves declaring any poignant ministry moment "prophetic" where His manifest presence is elevated and people are deeply affected.

Elders and believers who have experienced corporate prophetic ministry readily admit there are discernible differences in the impact of different prophetic messages people share. They will always label the ones where God's manifest presence was significantly heightened during or right after the sharing as "prophetic."

Some call it *anointing,* other's *blessing* or *empowerment,* but when any vocal ministry (such as "a hymn, a lesson, a revelation, a tongue, or an interpretation" as in 1 Cor. 14:26) comes forth in the corporate gathering of saints in a manner that leaves them declaring "God is really among you," that moment is immediately raised to the level of "prophetic." Not just because they were encouraged by hearing what they wanted to hear, but because God came near and that is what brings the edification.

As leaders, we must be careful not to lower our expectation of the prophetic to positive platitudes, psychic clairvoyance, and pious sentimentality that entirely misses the point of the gift— the ushering in of His manifest presence among us.

Our true encouragement from the prophetic is being reminded of His sovereignty, not our self-worth. And nothing communicates His sovereignty more than His manifest presence in our midst.

Therefore, we must courageously go deeper in our pursuit of prophecy that edifies, not because it talks about our needs alone or creates emotionalism, but because we experience God's manifest presence and we are changed.

If He dwells in us, why do need Him to manifest His presence among us?

Any pursuit of corporate prophetic ministry should be to echo Moses' plea on the mountain before God in Exodus 33:15-16 (NIV), "If your Presence does not go with us, do not send us up from here...What else will distinguish me and your people from all the other people on the face of the earth?"

When Moses was asking God's presence to go with them, it wasn't that God wasn't already omnipresent, in every place, in every moment. He was drawing attention to God's blessing, or favor, resting upon them as a people.

There is a difference between God being everywhere at once, and when His presence is manifestly felt. He is everywhere in the world, but His blessing is toward His Church. One has to do with His universal omnipresence; the other has to do with His favor.

When we are filled with His Spirit as believers, we are anointed, filled with His Holy Spirit. We are repositioned as adopted sons and daughters, and He is with us. However, there is also subsequent favor and blessing that comes upon us when the Holy Spirit manifests His presence among us.

In the book of Acts, He repeatedly fills and manifests His presence when asked (Acts 2:4, 4:8, 13:52, 19:6). We can experience this during times of preaching, prayer, worship, or any other time we determine to make Jesus the focus of our hearts.

To experience His Spirit's manifest presence in the corporate gathering, the leaders must be continually asking, praying, and inviting Him to come. Not only as He is omnipresent in that moment, but also as He is manifest among us openly through gifts, infilling, peace, and power.

As Moses declared, it's this manifestation of His Spirit that reveals how we are distinguished from all other peoples on the face of the earth.

Chapter 19

Pursuing True Prophetic Ministry

Pastors should tell their teams they are looking for Jesus and His work, as the primary spirit (or focus) of prophecy. "For the testimony of Jesus is the spirit of prophecy" (Rev. 19:10). When the people's hearts are inclined to see and experience Jesus, the Holy Spirit will reveal Him and the glorious hope of the gospel through prophecy. This will result in a greater revelation of HIM.

Revealing HIM and the Gospel in Prophecy

I believe the Holy Spirit gave me a simple acronym that provides a good picture of Jesus-focused prophetic content.

HIM: Holiness, Immutability, Majesty

These words represent some of His most important attributes that should be evident in all our prophetic ministry content. It doesn't mean these exact words need to be used, but the essence of their meaning should be central to any prophecy's doctrinal theme. If we understand the Spirit's only desire is to manifest Jesus among us, then we must realize that every revelation we call "prophetic" will be about HIM.

Holiness - He is not like us.

"Sacred, set apart, pure in the extreme" is *what holiness* means. He is entirely "other." We are not like Him, because He

194 RECLAIMING PROPHECY / Slack

is separate. Entirely pure, good, and righteous. There is none like Him, nor will there ever be. His thoughts and ways are not like ours; therefore Him revealing His Holiness is appropriate and continually necessary to inform a right perspective of Him. He wants to show us what He is like, and it has little in common with how we often see Him. In similar fashion, He wants to reveal His goodness to us, which is entirely different from how we react toward others or ourselves.

This is why I emphasized that holiness reflected in prophecy will highlight the clear difference between Him and us; He is not like us. Our prophecy must never fashion Him into our image of who He is or what we want Him to be for us.

We must not allow how we feel about a situation, or the Church, to come into our message. We must allow Him to be and say who He is through us without hesitation or reservation. The Church's greatest need is not getting more of what they want from Him; it's getting to see Him more and more as He is to us, in us, and through us.

Therefore, we should expect the Holy Spirit to speak faithfully of His attributes in the prophetic and not be entirely focused on our needs, failures, and wants. The prophetic should be God-centered and about what He wants.

True prophecy of His Holiness reveals who He is, as He is. This will bring more edification than we could ever ask for or imagine.

Immutability - He does not change

"Unchanging; not capable of, or susceptible to, change" is the meaning of *immutability*. It's incredibly important that the people of God know He is the same yesterday, today, and forever, and while their circumstances will fade, His love, His promises, and His steadfast faithfulness will never fail.

Our prophetic content must not waver at any point or presume He would react as we do. In Malachi 3:6, He tells us, "For I the Lord do not change," therefore any true prophecy must not fail in declaring the unchanging nature of who He is at all times, even in adversity.

Who is He, we ask?

He gave us a pretty good idea where to start in Exodus 34:6-7 (NIV) when He introduced himself as, "The Lord, the Lord, the compassionate and gracious God, slow to anger, abounding in love and faithfulness, maintaining love to thousands, and forgiving wickedness, rebellion and sin."

We cannot improve on the gospel as the example we point to of God's unchanging love and faithfulness. We can expect the Holy Spirit to be redundant about His passion to remind us of His unchanging nature through the gospel. He won't brood over our issues or change because things get hard for us; He will reveal His immutable, unchanging nature to the church through the gospel in the prophetic.

As "the testimony of Jesus is the spirit of prophecy," His changeless nature must inhabit its every line. Hebrews 13:8 tells us, "Jesus Christ is the same yesterday, today, and forever."

Majesty - He is sovereign

"Sovereign power, authority, and greatness of splendor" is the definition of *majesty*. God is sovereign and supreme over all things. He is The King.

Our prophetic messages must always point to His absolute sovereign control of all things. We must never offer prophetic ministry that strays from declaring His majesty in everything. Even when we face adversity and difficulty, our prophetic message will not change regarding His control and wonderful plan for our lives.

Prophetic people can expect the Holy Spirit to declare and reveal His sovereign control. We should interpret and apply what we hear and see in terms of that sovereignty over all things.

Prophetic people are primarily heralds of His sovereignty, not man's significance. He will not ignore our need, but He won't make much of it either.

We often make much of ourselves with all our needs, but true prophecy should meet the only need any of us have, to make much of Him.

The Gospel

Jesus' finished work on the cross and subsequent resurrection in victory over death is the prophetic message of God toward man, dwelling in man, and working through man. There is no prophecy more edifying than to speak of Him is who greater than all, who made the greatest of all sacrifices for us.

The gospel is the pinnacle of His greatest work throughout History. It's the story that must be told over and over in every way possible. Prophetic ministry should declare Christ's words, "It is finished" over His Church as a reminder of the immeasurable debt He paid on our behalf. Prophecy should cry out to the weary heart to have hope because of what the gospel provided. It should speak of great and precious promises that belong to the church in the inheritance purchased by our Savior's blood.

The gifts and manifestations of Spirit are the declaration of Christ, "It is finished," propelled through time and space to address any situation and circumstance we find ourselves in today. —Lewis Seifert

Prophetic people will never exhaust the ways the Spirit can saturate their prophetic ministry with the gospel, and that must be their primary passion. For it's in the message of Christ crucified and risen again where the Spirit manifests Himself and demonstrates His power (1 Cor. 2:2-4).

Where prophecy initiated by the Spirit exalts and honors Jesus, He will manifest His power and edify the church to confirm His voice. The Holy Spirit recognizes his own voice and will validate His message in the hearers. But as soon as the message ceases to be anchored in the gospel and person of Jesus Christ, it becomes man-centered and felt-needs focused. This is where a great deal of well-intentioned prophetic ministry loses its moorings to Scripture and can manifest more of man's imagination than the Spirit's impartation.

The gospel is the power of God to those who are being

saved (1 Cor.1:18). Any expression of the power of the Spirit has as its preeminent motive the message of the gospel. It is why He does what He does. The gospel is Father's will done through the Savior and being done through us by the Holy Spirit.

Chapter 20

Exploring Vocal Ministry in the Corporate Gathering

"What then, brothers? When you come together, each one has a hymn, a lesson, a revelation, a tongue, or an interpretation. Let all things be done for building up." (1 Cor.14:26)

In this verse, Paul declares the five types of vocal ministry that members should contribute during the corporate gathering of believers: a hymn, a lesson, a revelation, a tongue, or an interpretation.

By reviewing the spectrum of corporate vocal ministry and protocol in 1 Cor. 14:26 and following, we can understand better where the gift of prophecy fits specifically in the order of service. This will increase our faith in the Spirit to manifest Himself in broader vocal ministry we hope to also experience in a prophetic way.

Vocal Ministry Protocol in the Congregation

Where permitted by elders in the congregational gathering, vocal ministry is generally shared in two formats:

Open congregational sharing

This is when the elders provide planned instrumental or silent pauses during worship and prayer times, encouraging members to share aloud from their seats what God may be putting on their hearts.

Some churches prefer this approach as it is seen to be more dependent on the Holy Spirit in the gathering of the believers. And their church may not be large enough to warrant use of a microphone.

This method can present challenges for the elders if it is not done in a decent and orderly fashion. Also, there can be confusion if two people begin talking at the same time, two people's message themes are contradictory, or any message is not deemed to be from the Lord. So, it's important that instructions are provided by the elders regularly for how ministry should be done corporately in this manner.

Other churches, seeking to avoid some of those potential pitfalls, will use a ministry microphone for their more formal gatherings while reserving open congregational sharing in smaller group settings, such as care groups, prayer meetings, and less formal teaching gatherings of the believers.

There is still a need for the leaders present in any gathering to provide agreement or correction, or to invite any Spirit-led response.

Ministry microphone

In larger church gatherings, or more formal sessions, some elders will provide a microphone on a stand in some consistent, recognized position in the meeting room that is overseen by a pastor or recognized prophetic minister. During these times, members sensing a message or vision from the Lord that is for more than just them will bring it to the elder(s) at the microphone.

The leaders present will review it briefly for doctrinal accuracy, Holy Spirit timing and witness, continuity with current direction of the service, and accountability of the intended delivery.

This method, while avoiding some of the potentially confusing issues of open congregational sharing, could intimidate members from coming forward, delay the Spirit's timing for when He wanted a word delivered, and even quench the Spirit from moving. All because so little is approved and allowed to be shared.

This method asks members to be very vulnerable and courageous, so this approach must be filled with great encouragement to those who come. It must also include compassionate patience while someone tries to share what they are hearing from the Lord over the worship music and singing.

From an elder perspective, this clearly appears a superior method to avoid open congregational confusion, but speaking from experience in submitting to this model, it can be just as hindering to the work of the Spirit if not administrated in an engaging, faith-filled manner between the members and elders.

I maintain that dependence on the Spirit is measured in the heart of the elders and people, not in the methods used. Each elder team should determine what's best for their church's expression of the Spirit's ministry and must create a wide path for the Spirit to manifest in gatherings through vocal expression.

While I personally believe the ministry microphone is best in the church's main congregational gathering, the elders should regularly and publicly provide encouragement, faith, and clear instruction as to what is expected from those who come with something to share. This helps people from losing heart in coming forward or being repeatedly turned away because it doesn't meet criteria they don't understand. This doesn't mean everyone will always get to share, but there should be a reasonable framework of clarity, compassion, and feedback that serves the members.

Finally, it's entirely on the elders to make sure they regularly encourage the people who operate in the gifts to be active in any congregational gathering the leadership team deems appropriate, before, during, and after the meetings. If the sole focus of our gathering is singing, announcements, and preaching, the church can default to becoming spectators, not Spirit-led saints.

Let's take a deeper look at each corporate vocal ministry expression to better understand how we, as elders, can serve our members in administrating the gifts.

Vocal Ministry Gifts

Hymn

This is a prophetic song sung aloud before the congregation as the Spirit leads. It's often labeled prophetic by the manner in which God's presence manifests through it.

It can be a song revealed line by line to the singer as they sing, or one given to the singer ahead of time and written down. It can also be a known worship song or hymn they were directed to sing at a particular moment in time.

When the Church is gathered, the Father loves to be among His people and sing over them:

"The LORD your God is in your midst, a mighty one who will save; he will rejoice over you with gladness; he will quiet you by his love; he will exult over you with loud singing." (Zephaniah 3:17, emphasis mine)

Paul exhorts us to "be filled with the Spirit, addressing one another in psalms and hymns and spiritual songs, singing and making melody to the Lord with your heart" (Eph. 5:18b-19).

There is a scriptural command to sing to the Church as one of the fruits of the ongoing infilling of the Holy Spirit toward the people of God.

The true prophetic song or well-timed hymn brings great encouragement and comfort to His people because God's presence will manifest mightily.

Discerning and directing the delivery:

The prophetic songs will vary, but a new song will usually be a few verses and include a repeating chorus. If the member has a song to be sung in a tongue, as we are instructed, we will have the person stand nearby and wait to see if anyone comes forward with an interpretation. (See tongue/interpretation below.)

When there is a brand new song offered during worship or during a ministry moment, the member will begin singing and usually the worship leader will identify the key in which the song is being sung and play a chord progression as they feel led to back up the singer. If there is no worship leader or instrument, then the singer is on his or her own for the key.

If the new song comes from a member of the worship team playing an instrument, they can lead out in the chords and key they feel the Lord is giving them. If it's a song or hymn already known to the church, it will follow the same process.

If the elders permit open congregational sharing in the corporate gathering without a ministry microphone, there should be pauses during corporate worship and prayer times where people are encouraged to share what they feel the Lord has given to them. Once shared, it's important for the leaders to publicly respond to what has been shared to either validate or bring adjustment for the benefit of the church.

If there is a ministry microphone, the member will alert the elder(s) that they believe they have a song from the Lord, or wish to sing a known hymn, and will give them a sense of its purpose and direction. It's also very helpful for them to share a few lines of the song they feel are the theme of the message.

This step will increase faith in the leaders for the message coming forth and prompt them to prepare a time of response to what the Holy Spirit is doing.

Lesson (or "doctrine" in KJV)

A lesson is a brief exhortation or mini-teaching of doctrinal truth from Scripture that applies at a specific moment of worship, or during an administrated time of corporate prayer, that builds up the church.

The lesson will be a revelatory application of a truth from Scripture or something regarding His attributes. It may include reference to the unchangeable work of the gospel and how He will continue to be faithful and in control of all things. Though typically driven by a Scripture, it could include a picture analogy or metaphor with application as well. Regardless, it will be primarily exhorting and edifying.

This type of vocal expression runs right next to the more

specific gift of prophecy (revelation), because it involves a measure of revelatory application tied to what they feel God is saying from Scripture, the ultimate prophetic Word.

In fact, a lesson being shared can easily turn into a prophetic utterance, and even have a prophetic empowerment. One of my pastors ministers regularly this way. He will begin with a clearly exhorting lesson from Scripture, and while he is sharing, it will transition to what he feels he is receiving directly from the Spirit in the moment prophetically. (See methods of prophecy below.)

Paul's priority wasn't delineation of the gifts; it was edification from God's manifest presence through the gifts. If the message was delivered intelligibly while building up the Body of Christ through God's manifest presence, then the objective was achieved.

These distinctions between gifts are intended to provide the elders with categories to test the various manifestations for their potential to build up the Body of Christ through the manifestation of the Spirit. The labels provide contexts for vocal ministry while diminishing the temptation to legalistic rules, rituals, or traditions.

Discerning and directing the delivery:

The key points for the speaker to remember when there is a lesson to give would be the same as prophecy: precise and concise. The precision, brevity, and clarity of the delivery are all measures of the Spirit's influence on the speaker.

If the elders permit open congregational sharing of vocal expressions during worship or prayer times in the corporate gathering, there should be built-in pauses between songs and encouragement offered by the leaders for anyone who may sense something from the Lord to share.

At the ministry microphone, the speaker will share the Scripture and the essence of the revelatory application they have received. They want to include any pertinent words, analogies, or metaphors they sense the Spirit of God provided to confirm their message.

Revelation

Revelation is considered within the scope of prophecy because Paul references it as such in First Corinthians 14:29-30: "Two or three prophets should speak, and the others should weigh carefully what is said. And if a revelation comes to someone who is sitting down, the first speaker should stop." Also, any revelation shared by the Spirit is God prophesying Himself among us, His eternal perspective for us, and His promises to us (1 Cor. 14:25).

The prophetic message can be delivered in many different ways as discussed later in Appendix A, but for it to be shared corporately, it must be clear, concise, and edifying.

This revelation is not equal to Scripture, but rather is to be tested by Scripture for its truth and should only be acted on if there is faith and confirmation in the believer's own heart. Though many prophecies are conditional, no prophetic message is binding on any believer to obey it as Scripture.

Prophecy is not about clairvoyance or psychic ability, as those things draw attention to the speaker, but prophecy should herald the manifest presence of God in our midst and bring Him glory.

All revelation in prophetic ministry is to prophesy HIM (1 Cor. 14:25). If His presence is manifest, the people of God will be encouraged, edified, and comforted (1 Cor. 14:3).

Discerning and directing the delivery:

If the elders permit open congregational sharing of prophetic ministry during worship or prayer times in the corporate gathering, there should be built-in pauses between songs and encouragement offered by the leaders for anyone who may sense something from the Lord.

At the ministry microphone, we ask individuals to share briefly what they are getting from the Spirit—words to be spoken or a vision with interpretation and application. If it's words, and it's written down, we will read what they brought.

If they feel it's to be delivered in a streamed or "prompted" manner as they receive it (see types of prophecy in Appendix A) we ask them to give us the theme of the message and who, if any particular group, it might be directed toward. If it's a vision with an interpretation/application, we ask for an overview of the vision, what it means, and who, if any particular group, it might be directed toward.

We would also ask them to make sure they begin the delivery of the prompted prophetic message with, "I believe the Lord would say...." This leaves room for assessment of the message, while assuring the hearers that we understand what is being shared is not equal to Scripture.

Once the prophetic messages begin coming forward, we ask the Holy Spirit to provide the elder(s) direction as to what words will be shared, and in what order. Typically, multiple words that are similar are confirmation of what the Spirit seems to be doing. At that point, we consider the clarity of the content presented, the proven experience of the messengers, and which messages best complement one another.

As in the exhortation of sharing a lesson, prophecy should be precise, concise, and clear, especially if it is shared extemporaneously. One other important evidence of the Spirit in sharing a prophetic message is boldness.

It's very important that anyone preparing to share something from the Spirit allow the empowering boldness of the Spirit to infuse their speech. Words shared timidly lack the affirming witness of the Holy Spirit. It's not just the volume of the voice that determines boldness, but the conviction present in the clarity and confidence with which it's shared.

None of what is shared is considered to be equal to Scripture in authority, but rather is to be tested by Scripture to ensure what is shared is consistent with biblical truth (1 Thess. 5:19-21).

Following any ministry time, elders should get with those who brought words forward but weren't permitted to share them. In most cases, there is a need to adjust their perception of what was prophetic in that moment, their wording of the message, or their timing with regard to the service direction.

At times, what members share will confirm what the Holy

Spirit is already doing. They will be encouraged in that way and be asked to hold on to what they have received or to ask God if what they have might be for a specific person.

If the timing or content needs clarity, the leaders present at the microphone will offer brief feedback and encouragement, asking the member to seek God for more, write down what they are getting, or return when it's clearer.

Tongue

An utterance in an unknown tongue. A spirit-infused declaration of praise to God in a manner we neither understand with our mind nor can do on our own. Tongues are used in multiple ways by the Holy Spirit in Scripture. He uses our tongue to speak in languages that others can understand, even though we cannot in the moment. ("We hear them declaring the wonders of God in our own tongues!"—Acts 2:11 NIV .)

He uses our tongue to speak in a language that edifies our spirits and builds our faith in prayer (1 Cor. 14:4; Jude 20). Finally, He uses our tongue to prophesy, speak praises, and offer thanks to God with an interpretation for edification of His gathered Church (1 Cor. 14:5, 16-17; Acts 2:11).

Jesus told us that believers would speak in new tongues in Mark 16:17. Tongues are a willing surrender of one's tongue, reputation, and ownership of communication to the Holy Spirit, and are therefore a wonderful demonstration of the lordship of Jesus Christ in our lives.

This is why Paul declared we should not forbid speaking in tongues, because no one can prophesy, praise, and thank the Father through us like the Holy Spirit.

The objective of a tongue and interpretation is to manifest His sovereign involvement in our gathering, while demonstrating our utter dependence on Him.

Discerning and directing the delivery:

If the elders permit open congregational sharing of tongues during worship or prayer times in the corporate gathering, there should be built-in pauses between songs and encouragement offered by the leaders for anyone who may sense something from the Lord. If there is a tongue, there should be an intentional or instrumental pause to await an interpretation to come.

At the ministry microphone, when a person brings a "tongue" message forward, we will encourage them to stand nearby as we patiently wait for the Spirit to confirm His work by sending someone up with the interpretation. The person with the tongue can certainly interpret if they feel led, but if not, we will wait to see if the Spirit brings someone forward with an interpretation. I believe it's appropriate for leadership to communicate faith to the congregation by stating that a tongue has come forward and they are awaiting an interpretation. If no one comes forward to interpret, we will typically encourage the member with the tongue who came forward in obedience, but they will not be allowed to share what they have.

If the tongue is permitted by leadership to be shared without a confirmed interpretation beforehand, the leadership should pause and alert the church that they are awaiting an interpretation. If no interpretation comes forward, then the leadership should explain that while we trust God for the Spirit's work in our midst, if there is no interpretation, they are to disregard the tongue that came forth.

If the person spoke the tongue out in a meeting without leadership approval, and no interpretation comes, it may be appropriate to visit with them and discuss the Scriptural mandate for order and the need for an interpretation to edify the church.

Interpretation

It can be a spirit-led expression of praises and thanksgiving to God or a direct prophetic message shared. Although there is a tongue used by the Spirit that some can understand in their own language, this corporate application of the gift shared as an interpretation is not typically a direct translation of the tongue.

This is because there probably aren't words in English that are the same as the Spirit used. It's a Spirit-led interpretation of the message given in tongues that is designed to edify, exhort, and comfort the Church.

Even in the case of those hearing the "wonders of God in our own language," it is likely the Spirit is working miraculously in the hearers to understand as an interpreted translation in their own languages, because the speaker is not aware of what they are saying.

And in the case of the Acts 2:11 crowd, there were many nationalities present, while many different tongues were being spoken, making it impossible to distinguish which tongue being spoken was being translated to the hearers.

It was the Holy Spirit opening their ears, in their language, in that moment, to understand what was being declared as a unique sign of His arrival at Pentecost. He was letting them understand what He came to do through these strange acting people—to declare the wonders of God! The speaker is only responsible to speak forth the tongue without understanding. The translation of the unknown language is entirely dependent upon the Spirit enabling the hearer to understand, and therefore we will never know how direct the translation is until we reach heaven.

Truth is, we probably couldn't pronounce much of the actual tongue-spoken words directly in our own language, and it is unlikely they would translate easily. We struggle to translate Spanish to English directly; how can we expect to translate an "angelic" language (1 Cor. 13)?

I think of interpretation as a more childlike utterance that interprets a much greater and more involved declaration of the Spirit toward God. He is declaring attributes of God we cannot fathom in our praise through tongues.

To encourage us following His proclamation in tongues, He does what any father would do when a child hears or sees their father doing something really interesting and wants to do it; He filters it down and lets us participate with Him as a child.

What may have been the Spirit's specific praise reference to the absolute immutability of His sovereignty over quantum-level concepts in galaxies we've never seen, He lets us agree with what He just said, but in terms we can understand and be edified by, "Father, you are sovereign in all this Universe..."

He goes off speaking of the Unspeakable as only He can, then He stops and takes our hand and says, "Now you go, and I'll help you." The Father is doubly honored in that moment, first by the Holy Spirit's declaration of His kingdom and majesty in tongues, and then through the interpretation of a former object of His wrath, who is now an adopted, redeemed sinner learning how to praise the Father through obedient surrender to the gift being manifested before the church.

This is also why Paul said, "Pray that you may interpret!" Why? Not just so the Church can be edified, but because we get the chance to see God more clearly in the praise of the Spirit through us.

We must not be troubled by the concept that we cannot translate His words directly, simply because He is not like us. Rather, we should rejoice that we get to participate in the Spirit's direct praise of our Great God!

Discerning and directing the delivery:

If the elders permit open congregational sharing of tongues and interpretation during worship or prayer times in the corporate gathering, there should be a built-in pause immediately following a given tongue for anyone who may sense they have the interpretation from the Lord.

If there is a ministry microphone, then the interpretation will be handled very much like a prophecy. We will have the speaker share the theme of the interpretation they are receiving. Remember that translation is up to the Spirit in the hearer's ears, not on the speaker. We are interpreting, not translating what the Spirit is giving us. Noting this as an interpretation is also important because of the imperfect nature of the human creature the message is coming through, and the fact that the inspiration is not equal to Scripture.

Is the interpreted tongue always in language directed toward God as praise, thanks, prayers, and declarations of the wonders of God, or can it be shared as a directed prophetic message toward the church?

In my humble view, I believe a true tongue from the Spirit so stirs the human spirit with faith that the prophetic is stirred as interpreted praises, prayers, and thanksgiving to God.

Faith is the fuel of prophecy (Rom. 12:6), and tongues stir faith (Jude 20), so prophecy is encouraged by the gift of tongues. But I will also say that a faith so stirred by the Holy Spirit by His words unknown to us, yet so compelling to our spirits, produces soul-emptying cries of praise, thanks, prayers, and declarations of His awesome wonders!

Like laughter and tears are so close they often crossover, I believe the power of tongues in the Holy Spirit stirs every fiber of our spirit to praise and prophesy the greatness of our God in equal measure.

The primary expression of interpretation based on my study of Scripture is as praises, prayers, thanksgiving, and declaring the wonders of God (1 Cor. 14:16-17; Acts 2:11). But, I would be remiss if I didn't admit that there are many times I've been stirred to prophesy after a tongue just as passionately. However, the desire to prophesy as a result of being stirred by a tongue doesn't necessarily mean it's the interpretation of the tongue.

There is more evidence for interpreted tongues to be shared as praises, prayers, thanksgiving, and declaring the wonders of God, but that alone isn't enough to suggest that limits the Spirit's ability to manifest as He wills.

Each church elder team must determine for themselves where they stand on the biblical mandate for content and direction of the words in an interpretation.

To suggest that the Spirit would prophesy by initiating it with a tongue contradicts Paul's assertion that prophecy edifies more effectively because it's intelligible in its delivery (1 Cor. 14:5). To now make the case that a prophecy given first in a tongue must now be interpreted to be edifying is both confusing and unfaithful to Paul's clear direction in the passage. It might be best for the elder team to clarify the Scriptural differences for those who are learning to filter what they are receiving from the Lord.

I would recommend an acknowledgment by the elders that prophecy is often stirred up by tongues through faith, but there is no Scriptural example for prophecy being an interpretation directly from a tongue. This is not legalism; it's about reducing confusion in the congregation concerning what they are hearing. If a tongue comes, they are expecting an interpretation. If a prophecy then comes as the interpretation, there will be questions about whether it was an interpretation or just a prophecy stirred by the tongue. The confusing order can hinder the edifying nature of the word.

Some would say that a praise, prayer, or thanksgiving interpretation doesn't speak to the church, so how is the church edified? I believe this question altogether misses the point of edification in vocal ministry. It's the manifest presence of God that accompanies the vocal ministry that edifies, not just the words being said. Whenever the name of Jesus is exalted, the Holy Spirit is likely to manifest His presence to edify. The manner of delivery can and will vary, but we are seeking His presence that accompanies the message as that which edifies.

This doesn't mean they cannot occur in the same meeting and be noted for what they are, tongues and prophecy. But direct interpretation should be administrated and affirmed as praise, prayers, and thanksgiving in words toward God.

Our fallback position for whatever is unclear with regard to the prophetic and vocal gifts is: We "see through a glass, darkly" (1 Cor. 13:12 KJV) to keep what He has revealed ever before us, "so with yourselves, since you are eager for manifestations of the Spirit, strive to excel in building up the church" (1 Cor. 14:12). We will see the church built up when our focus is on His manifest presence as the edifying reality.

The focus for whatever is allowed to be done by elders in the corporate gathering is to let it be done decently, in order, and always emanating from faith (Rom. 14:22-23).

Chapter 21

How Do We Discern If a Prophecy Is "Prophetic"?

"When the Spirit of truth comes, he will guide you into all the truth, for he will not speak on his own authority, but whatever he hears he will speak, and he will declare to you the things that are to come." (John 16:13)

"But the Helper, the Holy Spirit, whom the Father will send in my name, he will teach you all things and bring to your remembrance all that I have said to you." (John 14:26)

"But the one who prophesies speaks to people for their strengthening, encouraging and comfort." (1 Cor. 14:3 NIV)

"Do not quench the Spirit. Do not treat prophecies with contempt but test them all; hold on to what is good." (1 Thess. 5:19-21)

"If your gift is prophesying, then prophesy in accordance with your faith." (Rom. 12:6b NIV)

Prophecy is when a revelation comes forth in the form of a spoken word to the church or an individual. The original meaning of *prophecy* is to "speak forth" (*pro* = "forth" and *phemi* = "speak"). The implication from the Scriptural definition is that prophecy is reporting, or speaking, something one receives from God.

When someone shares a prophecy in the church, due to the risk of flawed human interpretation, the word is to be tested against the Scripture. Not everything shared in human words will be from God. This begs the question, if the New Testament prophetic process is flawed, and we have flawless Scripture as the ultimate prophecy, why bother encouraging it at all?

For the same reason pastors preach in a flawed and dependent manner—because we are commanded to do so by the admonishment to eagerly desire that we may prophesy.

In our feeble efforts to discern what is of God and what is of man in prophecy, we are regularly made aware of experiences where God seemed to be more present or among us in some messages over others. This is the essence of true prophetic ministry: the discernment of God's manifest presence in the delivery of the prophetic message. The more His presence is increased, the more "prophetic" it is to us.

Dissecting the many reasons for the differences of God's manifest presence on a prophetic message to His people would be impossible. However, in addition to the acronym of HIM mentioned earlier, a process of discerning the potential of a message is needed to bring a manifestation of His Presence among us.

Weighing the Corporate Message

Here are some questions we can ask, with establishing verses, for weighing the *corporate* "prophetic" message before, during, or after it's given in the gathering of the saints.

1)   Is it God-centered?

"When the Spirit of truth comes..." (John 16:13a)

"But the Helper, the Holy Spirit, whom the Father will send in my name..." (John 14:26a)

The bulk of the content must NOT be feelings-focused, sin-saturated, or man-centered. It can highlight God's awareness of our situation and isolate specific warnings, distractions, idolatry, or unbelief, but prophecy isn't just about how God will meet our needs or address our failure, it's God declaring who He is as a Father who is for us in the midst of our need and failure. Our highest encouragement, edification, and comfort come from God revealing Himself as mighty and powerful to address our needs or failures.

2)   Does it echo or agree with the truth of Scripture?

"...he will guide you into all the truth..." (John 16:13a) "...he will teach you all things and bring to your remembrance all that I have said to you." (John 14:26b)

The best test we have for evaluating what someone believes God has said is His own perfect words in the Scriptures. He will remind us of the truths of Scripture through revelatory exposition, interpretation, and application specific to our needs, in a perfectly timed fashion.

3)   Does it glorify Christ and His gospel provision?

"...he will not speak on his own authority..." (John 16:13b) "And Jesus came and said to them, 'All authority in heaven and on earth has been given to me.'" (Matt. 28:18)

Jesus holds all authority and speaks to His Church by the Father's will through the Holy Spirit. To understand the mystery of that process is beyond our capacity, but we know on whose authority the Holy Spirit speaks, and that should be clearly evident in the message. The redemptive hope of the finished work of Jesus Christ on our behalf through the gospel should be evident. It's not that the prophetic message needs to preach the gospel, but its threads should be obvious throughout.

4)   Is it strengthening, encouraging, or comforting?

"But the one who prophesies speaks to people for their

strengthening, encouraging and comfort." (1 Cor. 14:3 NIV)

Is there a sense that the message will build up the body of Christ? We must be careful to check for anything in the message that might have an overly sharp edge of harsh correction, condemnation, or disqualification. This doesn't mean there can't be a corrective element to a prophetic word, but the theme should be thoroughly redemptive, merciful, and hopeful.

Typically, some prophetic people experience great turmoil in being dealt with by the Holy Spirit. His purification process is, in a word, intense. In the absence of a strong, thriving application of the gospel in the prophetic person's heart, they can unwittingly allow some of their frustration, anger, or pain to seep into the prophetic message.

It's very difficult to prophesy the mercy and grace of God to the Church when the speaker feels they are being worked through challenging times in their own lives. The Holy Spirit is faithful and can use the prophetic mightily in the heart of brokenness.

We just need to monitor how their heart is interpreting and applying the revelations they receive and share with the church. God is never tired, irritable, upset, worried, or angry. He is Holy (unlike us), Immutable (unchanging), and Majestic (sovereign) at all times, and any prophetic message must carry that reality throughout.

5)   *Does it confirm something God has previously revealed?*

"...and bring to your remembrance all that I have said to you." (John 14:26)

The message can be confirming something heard, promised, or planned from God or experienced in the past. This can include things revealed to leadership, other prophetic persons, or the recipients of the message.

It can be something right in line with the planned worship songs, another prophecy shared by someone else, the preaching of the Word, or where the leadership was sensing the Holy Spirit would be directing the service.

The woman at the well (John 4:16-19) and Paul (Agabus' prophecy in Acts 21:11) both experienced being reminded of something that was only known by God or was revealed by God before it was shared prophetically. The reminder was used as sign that God was speaking in that moment.

Remember, prophecy is a sign that discloses the secrets of the heart and confirms that God really is among us (1 Cor. 14:25),

6)   Is it significantly predictive? Directive? Corrective?

"...and he will declare to you the things that are to come." (John 16:13c)

"For the Lord GOD does nothing without revealing his secret to his servants the prophets." (Amos 3:7)

God will reveal things that are to come to His prophetic people. When it is included in a prophetic message, it's just important that what is stated is clear and concise, so it can be measured and applied.

This is not an immediately measurable factor, so it should not be considered in weighing the immediate edifying and God-honoring prophetic nature of a word.

Paul wouldn't have suggested that the word could be weighed by the other prophets when it is delivered if the predictive nature of the word were a requirement for authenticity in the moment. If it is predicting something better left unsaid in the moment, then it might be best to hold off on having that part shared publicly.

This should be determined by the leadership at the microphone. In any discussion of predictive prophecy given, I would encourage careful handling and pre-submission of those words, especially those regarding marriage, mortality, and maternity, especially in any individual prophetic context.

If the prophetic context doesn't allow for submission to anyone in the moment, then I would counsel any prophetic person to submit any predictive component of the word separate from the main content and prefaced with words like, "What I'm about to say is subject to His timing and will, but I believe He showed me that..."

If the word contains significant directives that are not consistent with Scripture, that suggest performance as required for God's blessing, or recommend the church elders take a specific course of action, I would recommend those words be submitted directly to the elder team and not be shared publicly. If they choose to share those words after they are read, then that is up to them and the Spirit's direction.

The goal is not control, but rather pastorally managing the flow of information to assist with communication and clarification of anything that might be confusing to the members. Directive words carry a measure of authority and should be prayed about at the elder level before anything is shared with the local church.

Finally, any words that are significantly corrective should be handled like directive words. The reason for this is that corrective words project a measure of authority as directive ones do. It's on the elder team to determine what, if any of the observations, they will lead the church to consider.

Significantly predictive, directive, and corrective words all potentially make a claim to authority on the elder team and the local church from the Lord. These types of words should typically come from the prophet/prophetess and should be edifying to the leadership on that level. It's up to the leadership to discern what will be edifying to the church from what is shared with them.

7)   *Is the potential speaker known to the congregation or recognized by another church as a believer who is of good character?*

In a ministry microphone setting, when discerning whether the elders will permit a prophetic word to come forth to the congregation, there is certainly a need to evaluate the potential speaker. If the person is not known to the elder or prophetic ministers, it makes the prospect of releasing them to share with the church significantly more difficult.

Does this mean we never let a visitor prophesy? No, it

just means the elder and prophetic ministers need to assess the message and planned delivery method more carefully to ensure they have a clear understanding of what will be said and how. Further, if a visitor struggles with submitting their word to the leadership, it is a clear indicator that they should not share it.

A member in good standing and character coming forward to share something is certainly going to present a more compelling messenger than someone just coming in for the first time. The objective isn't to be exclusive, but rather diligent to consider each point more carefully to qualify the person and the prophetic message.

In an open congregational setting, the message will need to be judged on its own merit by the leadership and responded to accordingly as the Spirit leads.

8)   *Is there faith for the content and timing of the message in the speaker, leadership, and believers (the prophetic chain)?*

"If your gift is prophesying, then prophesy in accordance with your faith." (Rom. 12:6)

A qualified New Testament congregational prophetic word would be an expression revealed by the Holy Spirit through the prophetic "chain." Like a series of links in a chain, He will connect all the elements of faith needed to communicate His heart.

He will influence the speaker's mind and spirit THROUGH faith, approve the message the leadership assesses IN faith, share through the speaker WITH faith, and insure the word is received BY faith.

Faith must saturate every link of the prophetic chain. It requires the speakers, leadership, and believers are "in faith" for what God is doing in the prophetic moment. If at any step faith is not present, the chain will break and the ministry will either not come forth or not edify the body.

The central, and strongest, link of faith for this ministry in the congregational prophetic chain is the leadership. They must influence both the speakers and believers to receive what God has for His Church in this ministry.

For this chain to be consistently strengthened with faith in our hearts as leaders, we need to be able to discern what the Holy Spirit is saying and doing.

The Three Tuning Forks of Discerning Faith in the Prophetic

It may be difficult to recall all the questions asked above about weighing a possible prophetic word, so here is an express version of the process above I've found helpful for discerning, or testing, the message.

The word

The prophetic message may not be a Bible verse, but whatever point is made or shared should reverberate, or echo, the truth of Scripture. It should carry the unmistakable, inerrant, published tenor of the Holy Spirit's canon. Like striking a tuning fork in the spirits of all present to hear, the message's tone should match the key, or pitch, of the fork (Holy Scripture, the "Word" of Christ) in every way.

The witness

Additionally, every believer, whether they realize it or not, knows what the Holy Spirit sounds like in their hearts. Romans 8:15 (NIV) declares that we have a tuning fork in our spirits through the witness of our "sonship" by the Spirit. When we hear something that witnesses deep in us as the Holy Spirit speaking, our spirits cry out, "Abba, Father," and we are undone with love for Him.

When we hear the Holy Spirit speaking, there is an agreement that floods our spirit with the desire to worship and draw near to the Father. True prophetic ministry produces an intimacy and affection for God. There is a "knowing that we know" that is neither explainable, nor repeatable in ourselves. It's a witness of sonship that only the Spirit can give. True prophetic ministry sounds like a gentle Father bending down to talk kindly and mercifully to His children.

The weight

There is one richer tuning fork to strike in listening for the true prophetic that we may not realize we know in our spirits. Some call it the anointing; I call it the "weight."

We know what truth sounds like from the Scripture, and we know what the Father looks like to His children from the witness of the Spirit in sonship, but the Scripture tells us that we can know what the "weight" of the kingdom of God feels like when it comes in our midst.

Romans 14:17 tells us what the kingdom of God feels like when it comes, and therefore what a true prophetic message should feel like: "For the kingdom of God is not a matter of eating and drinking but of righteousness and peace and joy in the Holy Spirit."

Any prophecy spoken from the kingdom of God by the Holy Spirit should have the recognizable attributes of His absolute *righteousness,* sentences dripping with the hope of the gospel of our *peace*, and floods of indescribable *joy* of His eternal perspective and sovereignty over our circumstances.

It's a sense beyond our senses that has a substance of heaviness or weight. It's not a burden, but a stunning arrival of Someone who is in all ways, more. Like a captivating and overwhelming awareness of His sudden, and wonderful, nearness.

In true prophetic utterance, God delights to be among His people, and where He is the weight of His kingdom is revealed in righteousness, peace, and joy.

This is the atmosphere of Heaven inhabiting the moment, the room and our spirits through an unmistakable prophetic declaration of HIM.

In these moments, when His weight is evident, the prophetic becomes much more than a person speaking about God into a microphone. We suddenly recognize the sovereignty of God rising to meet our gaze, and our souls leap at the presence of Heaven filling our hearts!

All at once, the speaker disappears from view, the kingdom of Heaven explodes into focus, and we fall down under the weight of unimaginable glory exclaiming loudly, "God is really among us!"

Leading a Corporate Response to the Spirit's Vocal Ministry

If the elders or worship leader sense a message shared came from the Holy Spirit, they should lead the congregational response immediately following it.

This is so everyone can understand the best way to process what came forth. Visitors need to understand what just happened and members want to benefit from a validating witness of leadership. This response could include, but is not limited to the following:

1)   Exhorting the congregation to apply the prophetic message personally

Consider how the Holy Spirit may be applying this message to them using additional Scripture or providing verbal affirmation of the Spirit's presence to meet the particular theme mentioned.

2)   Leading the entire congregation in a prayer for what was addressed in the message delivered

This could be a corporate moment of repentance, supplication, or intercession for the hearts of the church to experience more of God's grace related to the prophetic message.

3)   Lead in a time of ministry by asking for individuals to acknowledge if the prophecy spoke to them

Members can raise their hands and have nearby members gather around them to pray for them, or the elder(s) could ask the individuals who raised their hands to come to the front of the building as a step of faith and humility and pray for them as a group or individually with other leaders assisting. This would be more common when there is a heightened sense of urgency to focus on this group in prayer for things like healing, empowerment for calling, challenging needs, or significant comforting.

4)   *The elder(s) could sense the Holy Spirit, through the prophecy, or in response, sending the entire planned service schedule in a new direction*

This could involve many variations of what was already stated, extended prayer for the Spirit-led needs of the church, or an entirely different preaching plan.

These are some generic ways we've been led by the Spirit to respond, but each elder team should seek the Lord for what serves to build up their local church. The response should be just as Spirit-led in the elders as the message was in coming forth. The only stipulation for any of it is that it be done decently and in order so that all may be encouraged.

Chapter 22

An Appeal to Pastors

First, I want to thank you for reading this book. It tells me something of your desire to understand the nuances of a ministry that you believe has merit but has oft been misused and maligned. Hopefully, it will encourage your faith to consider prophetic ministry afresh for your church.

I would like to ask for your help on behalf of those of us who are not called to be pastors but sense a call to serve the Church in prophetic ministry.

Please engage us relationally and tell us how we can serve you best with our gifts. From the first day we indicate the stirring of the Spirit of prophecy in our hearts, guide us in what would help you most in administrating that ministry. You are reading this, so obviously you intend to do something with it. Tell us what you have faith for today in the prophetic and what you hope for in the future. This will let us know you are eager for our gift to grow, you want the church to be encouraged, and that we can confidently submit to your leadership for what makes sense now.

Please don't be intimidated or put off by our words or manner. We really are not all we tend to project sometimes. It's just that we often struggle with thinking we are just a "little" better because we heard something from the Spirit that others did not. We should know better, but you can help us with that. Please be patient with us.

We really do want to serve the church, but being used with

such a powerful and public gift like this can really tempt our desire for approval, validation, or position. We need feedback of a loving nature, corrective where necessary and appreciative where appropriate.

Really listen to us when we talk. We aren't always going to want to serve prophetically as we are particularly prone to discouragement, self-pity, and selfish ambition. One minute we are ready to take the hill, the next we just want to crawl in a hole and die. We can't hide it, but we will try to keep our chin up in every way possible. We will feign being strong and ready to be used, only to be sitting next to Elijah in the cave of our broken hearts, waiting for a certain death. We think so highly of our gift that we will seek to hear you tell us we're good because of our ministry. It isn't what we need from you. We need to hear the gospel again.

Watch our lives and families with us. We love to be used, but as a general rule, prophetic people aren't the greatest when it comes to dialing in our own character and responding humbly. The spiritual disciplines, intentional accountability, and commitment to a local church can be lost in our erroneous belief that because we hear God so clearly, He alone will be our guide. We desperately need the church to help us never seek validation for our gift, but only our character. Especially, keep a keen eye out for our spouses and kids. They can get shuffled to the periphery in our pursuit of your approval and validation for our gift. This can end up being to our shame, as our families cannot support our claim to be from God because of our hypocrisy.

We will light fires. Some that you will need to put out and some you will want to grow in others. Please keep us informed, as best you can, on which way the wind of our ministry is headed. We tend to lack the necessary meekness and understanding of the influence of this ministry on your work as a pastor.

We think nothing of sharing our word from the Lord in obedience, and we may not consider how it will affect what you are doing during the week in counseling and care for the people in your charge. Keep us posted when we are stepping beyond our God-ordained sphere of influence.

We often miss how you have the unenviable task of helping a person reconcile the lofty promise they may have heard on Sunday in a prophecy through us with the weaknesses you are working them through on Tuesday in your office. Help us learn how to position our words to allow room for the gospel to create something truly prophetic and encouraging about a person's growth in God.

We really do want to help. We just aren't always sure when to stop talking or when to start. We may make a mess with our enthusiasm or feel like a mess over our burden for purity in the church. We need grace upon grace and every ounce of compassion God can give you for us.

We need you to speak into our lives with the faith you have for what God can and will do in this ministry. We aren't always sure it's helpful, even though we act like it is. Our doubt comes from seeing through a glass darkly in our ministry, and that doesn't always lend itself to clarity of faith.

We know this ministry will never, and should never, supplant the preaching of the Word. It should never become a primary public expression of our life as the church in any way. However, where the Spirit seems to be leading, please initiate an inclusion of our passion to share something of God's heart with the church you have been given. It really matters to us to share what we believe the Lord has given us, even if we are only allowed to share a portion of it. If you can make time, it will really encourage our hearts.

When we share something, your feedback is critical. Even if you felt it wasn't all you hoped it would be. It matters that you care enough to help us see how we can grow in our faith and practice to be used. Tell us what helped and what didn't help that much and this will assist us in our future discernment and application

We would ask that you allow your faith to grow for us and this ministry in the same way you expect our faith to grow for what God will do through your ministry. We prophesy according to the proportion of our faith, and a large part of that faith to prophesy in and around the local church finds its validation in your faith for it in us.

Be patient with our failings and know that while we may challenge what you say or think things might have been better if you'd have done it another way, we are still learning of God's manifold grace as it is revealed in this ministry "in part."

Thank you in advance for your friendship, leadership, and the privilege of coming alongside you in the call of God on your life. Thank you for caring for our souls, even if we don't always thank you as we should. It is our joy to serve prophetically and hopefully hear as you will, "Well done, good and faithful servant."

Darin Slack
An aspiring servant in prophetic ministry

Acknowledgments

For God, My Savior, Jesus. My dearest Lord and King, there are no words. Only tears of gratefulness for Your unimaginable sacrifice to pay a debt I could not pay!

For God, My Heavenly Father. You have loved me with a steadfast love that has persuaded me that Your power is perfected in my weakness. Thank You for teaching me to let You love me so lavishly.

For God, the Holy Spirit. My faithful helper and the lover of my soul. Your voice only gets sweeter as I draw nearer to home. Thank You for whispering grace, wisdom, and courage over so many years to finish this work and the work You are finishing in me.

For Lesli, the unsurpassed delight of my earthly heart. You are the wife I dreamed of, prayed for, and received. Thank you for lovingly walking with me through the wilderness of God's faithful preparation. You are His love and grace personified in my life.

For my children, Matthew, Michael, Mark, Meaghan, and Meredith, the five richest deposits God has ever made in my life. Thank you for your understanding, support, and love through all my years of learning to value humility, love, and patience as a faithful father.

For Danny, Aron, Mike, Chip, and Chris, the Metro Life Church Leadership Team. Your faith, care, and patience for me, my family, and this gift's growth have been extraordinary. Thank you for thirty wonderful years.

For my many friends in Metro Life Church and on the Prophetic Team. Thank you for your faith and passion to see God glorified in His church through this gift. Your heart for one another is an example to me.

For Lewis. You are my true brother in life, in faith, and in ministry. This work doesn't happen if you weren't the incredibly faithful man you are. Thank you from my deepest affection for believing in me, and with me, for the glory of God to come through the prophetic.

For Debi. My true sister in Christ, you've inspired me to speak and write for His glory time and again. When my heart hurt the most, you kept writing God's promises in the journal of my soul. Thank you for prophesying His hope to me so I could finish this work.

For Pat, the Barnabas to my soul. Your unparalleled gift of encouragement and faith for what God would do, is doing, and has done is unmatched in all my Christian experience. You are a treasure of blessing in my life.

For Rob, the guiding voice in my writing head. You have expertly done what none have been able to do—you've made sense of my thoughts so others may benefit. Thank you for being used as a faithful filter of God's grace flowing through my life and words.

For Paul, the pastor who walked with me through this long road to completion. Your faithful words, edits, and insight have shaped my life and this work. Thank you for your kind friendship and letting us serve your church with our perspective on prophecy.

Appendix A

Prophetic Means and Methods

Just as the body of Christ has many parts, there are many ways in which the Holy Spirit manifests prophetic ministry. Regardless of delivery method, each message is still subject to the test of Scripture, the elders' and prophets' evaluation, and the witness of the Holy Spirit in the believers.

Prophetic people must be careful not to celebrate the uniqueness of how they are used, but rather continually rejoice in the gospel that made it possible for them to hear Him to encourage His Church through His manifest presence.

Each of the following descriptions is broadly written to allow for variations as the Spirit works through different people, places, and personalities. These can be in a corporate or individual context. There are no methods or formulas, only experience "guard railed" by Scripture.

In each description there are common non-negotiables of prophetic ministry that qualify them to be included for evaluation as "prophetic": the message is shared in an understandable way to the hearers and its content has the capacity to bring God's manifest presence in greater measure.

Its clarity to the hearers doesn't necessarily make it biblical or accurate, but intelligibility is a prerequisite explained in some detail through Paul's comparison to unintelligible tongues in 1 Corinthians 14.

It wasn't the strangeness of tongues as a gift, the fear of counterfeited tongues by the enemy, the disorderly noise that resulted, or the social awkwardness of tongue speaking in general that made Paul say things were out of order; it was just spoken in a language no one could understand and therefore couldn't be edifying to the church.

This is by no means an exhaustive list of His ways to prophesy. Also, the alliteration is not meant to be anything other than a means of quickly recalling these ideas for assistance in training others. You will undoubtedly recognize the inclusion of other gifts often associated with prophecy, such as Scripture reading, the word of wisdom, word of knowledge, and discerning of spirits. But simply listing the biblical gifts doesn't always clearly describe how they are being included in the Spirit's ministry practically. These contexts may provide more recognizable means that the Spirit uses.

For anyone seeking to be used prophetically, to build faith, the Holy Spirit will routinely change the delivery method they normally use to increase their dependence on Him. His power is made perfect in weakness (2 Cor. 12:9), not in lofty speech (1 Cor. 2:1).

Prophetic people must not become formulaic in their approach to the prophetic, but rather faithful to obey. The Holy Spirit will not be limited by superstitions, unbelief, and pride. Everyone needs to keep in "step with the Spirit" (Gal. 5:25) by allowing Him to expand their willingness to be used in different ways to ensure He receives every ounce of the glory.

Some Ways Believers Are Used in Prophecy:

1. "Prompted" prophecy (Acts 13:1-3, 21:11)

This is where a person will speak as if the Holy Spirit were speaking a brief message directly through them.

This message is "given as it is gotten." That means the speaker will typically have the first sentence or two of the word to begin, and in faith, as they are extemporaneously speaking, the Holy Spirit will impress the next words to say.

This prophetic flow can be preceded by the reading of a Scripture verse(s) that frames the theme of the message, but it isn't required. It could also be led with a brief description of a picture (see "picture" prophecy below) before it begins.

Practically, if the speaker has a preceding verse to share, they should share the verse and the Bible reference to provide a clear distinction between what is written and what they will be speaking.

If they have a picture, or vision, they should share the key elements of the picture they have received in plain language. When they have finished with the vision description or Bible verse, they need to set apart any prompted prophetic ministry coming next by saying something like, "I believe the Lord would say…"

There are some who feel they need to begin the flow with "Thus says the Lord" or "The Lord would say…" Humility suggests adjusting for flawed human interpretation while leaving room for others' evaluation by starting with, "I believe the Lord would say."

This allows the speaker to talk in their own plain words until they submit to what they believe is the flow of prompted ministry from the Holy Spirit. This sets a clear line between the types of the words to be weighed by the hearers. This humble step doesn't diminish the power of God; it serves to release it, while providing a context for pastoral follow-up and evaluation.

When the prompted message follows a tongue, this would be known as an interpretation. It can sound just like a normal prophecy to the church or as words directed to God in praise, prayer, thanksgiving, or declarations of His wonders.

These distinctions are as the Spirit wills and are still subject to the elders and prophets assessment.

Regardless, a prompted prophecy as an interpretation of a tongue is not usually a direct translation (unless God intends some hearers to understand it that way), will not necessarily be as many words as the tongue spoken, and must immediately follow the tongue given in the corporate gathering to ensure the church is edified (1 Cor. 14:28).

Prompted Quick Notes:
- Shared first-person, as the Lord spoke to the prophet, using *I*, *me*, and *my*
- This word is shared extemporaneously, or not memorized
- It may include a scripture verse(s) or vision shared before the message is shared

- Flow typically lasts thirty to ninety seconds; any more loses credibility
- Person sharing prophecy may get the gist of words to begin and a few sentences to start
- When it is prophetic, there will be an anointing that accompanies it
- It may also be an interpretation to a tongue that is spoken beforehand

2. "Paraphrased" prophecy (Acts 15:32, 11:28)

This is common in all contexts of prophetic ministry and is typically used more than the prompted method. There are some leaders who prefer this approach to the prompted prophecy to distance the speaker from appearing to speak directly for God.

Some people feel more in faith to explain what God has shown them and what they believe it means, rather than "stream" it as they speak. The speaker must be prepared to obey whatever the Spirit is giving direction and faith to do, while respecting the leadership's wishes.

As long as the message is clear and understandable, the content can be weighed by the leadership. This method of paraphrasing puts less pressure on the speaker to string together a message they don't fully know yet like prompted prophecy. Because they can pause in between thoughts to clarify what they are hearing inside, some just feel more comfortable speaking this way rather than as if God is directly speaking through them.

While it might require more faith for some people to operate in prompted prophecy if they are accustomed to a paraphrased approach, the reverse is also true if they are more comfortable with the Holy Spirit just streaming it live.

When the Spirit is moving in a believer's heart, He understands how they think and respond, as well as what delivery He prefers through them. He will usually direct the method He prefers a person use along with the message.

For those who prophesy more frequently, it's not uncommon to have the Holy Spirit use many approaches, with each one testing the faith of the speaker in a given situation. The anointing isn't on the believer's method, but rather it's on their faith and obedience to deliver it. Similarly, the method is never what makes a word prophetic; it's the Holy Spirit's anointing upon it.

This method is particularly common in individual prophetic ministry. It includes the use of the gifts of the word of wisdom, knowledge, and discerning of spirits. As in all prophetic ministry, the speaker must be careful to condense their sharing to the main points, seeking the Lord for the clearest interpretation and application possible.

This is why I recommend that a person sharing this way speak a bit slower, allowing pauses for the Spirit to increase unction, clarity, and specificity in the moment. If we speak too fast, we run the risk of missing what the Spirit wants to do in the ministry moment. Simultaneous hearing and speaking will take some practice, but it will be a wonderful way to minister in a very disarming, non-threatening tone to people.

We can simply share what we sense the Lord is showing us for someone in the course of normal conversation. If you want to add, "I really believe the Lord wants to bless you" or "I believe the Lord showed me some things about you," that is another way to start the flow of paraphrased prophecy.

What follows should be conversational, concise, and precise. It's not uncommon when stepping out in faith to share the first few things, for the Holy Spirit to quickly include additional insights and thoughts while we are speaking. We must be sensitive while we are sharing, as the Holy Spirit loves to use us to deliver good news to people.

Paraphrase Quick Notes:
- Speaker shares what they believe they heard from God in a clear, concise message
- Usually delivered as a series of direct statements in third-person language (*He*, *Him*, etc.)

3. "Picture" prophecy (Acts 21:11)

A "picture" prophecy is a vision followed by an interpretation/application in prompted, or paraphrased, format. The vision, or image(s), arrives through the visual part of the imagination like a flash across our minds. The vision can also come during sleep in the form of a dream. Whether in sleep or awake, the vision will usually prompt a stirring from the Holy Spirit to turn our attention to receiving more clarity, or the interpretation.

A dream will usually play out in full measure, and once recalled, the interpretation will be necessary at that point. However, when receiving a vision while awake, once the initial image appears, the Holy Spirit will typically render various parts of the picture/vision in greater detail. It may include additional elements, words written on objects in the picture, or a recurring action being shown like a video playing before us.

Because we see like we prophesy, "in part," we must patiently allow the Spirit to bring increasing clarity to the vision and not be in a hurry to receive the interpretation.

Early on in my prophetic experience with a picture or vision, I would mistakenly strive to understand every specific element and its purpose in the picture. Unfortunately, I would often end up in the flesh trying to do the Holy Spirit's job for Him. He would correct my striving effort, settle my restless childlike heart that was getting more confused by the moment, and patiently begin again. Eventually, He would help me understand what I was seeing and what it meant.

Imagine for a moment that the ocean is God's presence and you are keeping your head peacefully underwater for thirty seconds at a time before surfacing for a breath.

If we are waiting on the Spirit for clarity, it will be as if we are holding our breath and lowering our face into the water, peering into His depths and waiting patiently for His leading. Visibility will be difficult and we can only stay under for so long. Thirty to forty-five seconds would be about how long the average person can hold a breath, but that's also about how long we can sustain our focus on what God is showing us in the Spirit.

We need to train ourselves to stay "under" longer in God's presence, but at times, when I receive a prophetic word or picture from the Spirit, I feel like I am repeatedly surfacing to figuratively "catch my breath."

Like a child who can't settle down mentally, I am constantly clearing distractions and thoughts seeking to take me away from Him and what He is communicating. I can even be experiencing good thoughts, Scriptures, quick interpretations of what I'm seeing, attaching meaning from my own perspective. Even those "good" ideas need to be cleared like fog from the snorkel mask to allow the Holy Spirit to clarify my visibility.

Each time I return my focus onto the depth of what He was saying or showing, I ask Him to take me a little further and deeper into it. It's like opening an illustrated book to an image on a particular page, staring intently for a few moments, having it close, and then constantly reopening to that page to build out the full picture and its meaning. He is so patient to await my return and focus, and I can tell that it brings Him pleasure when I keep coming back.

This repetitive process of "looking" at the vision for clarity is best demonstrated by Daniel's description of his actions while receiving his vision of the four beasts and the Ancient of Days in Daniel 7:4, 6, 7, 9, 11, 13, and 21. It says in each verse that he "looked" repeatedly and/or "saw" something each time he did. There is a sense of the vision unfolding, or being revealed in greater measure, as we are faithful to focus deeper.

Discipline in picture prophecy is so important to not overwhelming ourselves or others with details and interpretations that may not matter. Never have the words "precise and concise" meant more than in picture prophecy. Let's be diligent to allow the Spirit to clear the fog from our swim mask, dive down a little deeper again, and let Him show us what He is doing before we rush to share what we think we've received.

When cuing up a vision ahead of a prophetic word to be shared corporately or individually, it's best to allow the gist of the picture to be sufficient and allow the Holy Spirit to expand on it for them when they seek Him on their own. We should offer a solid overview of the picture and cut to the chase of the message. We must avoid too many details to reduce confusion. The Holy Spirit will fill in the blanks for the hearer. We need to seek the Spirit for the appropriate amount of interpretation and application if He is giving one.

Picture Quick Notes:
- A vision or image accompanied by an interpretation/application
- Can be followed by a prompted or paraphrased prophecy
- Important to share clearly, but focus should be to get to the point succinctly
- Can be a description of what some are experiencing or are doing
- Application is up to the hearers and their sense of obedience to God
- A clear interpretation of the picture should be required to publicly share a corporate prophecy

4. *"Printed" prophecy (any of these methods written down)*

The only difference in this method of "printed" prophecy from all the others listed is that we are simply writing down everything the Spirit of God is revealing before we share it. This can take any of the forms of prophecy referenced in this section. This method effectively serves in many ways.

For prophetic ministry learning, it provides someone mentoring the prophetic person a clear feedback mechanism to speak from. It allows the overseeing leader the chance to know exactly what will be said, thus making it easier to "weigh." It provides a wonderful opportunity for post-delivery input from other prophetic ministers. Finally, it's a humble first step in proving our capacity to hear and obey the Lord.

While it certainly is not required, it demonstrates a measure of faith and preparation before the meeting, a willingness to submit to the authority present and a desire to improve in the use of the gift. It also reduces the pressure on the speaker in corporate sharing because it's already captured.

It's not the only method, but to strategically develop the gift in newer speakers, in more conservative settings where the gifts are less active, or in places where the potential speaker is not known to the leadership, this is a very humble and effective means of grace.

This is likely the best starting point for any church seeking to open the door to prophetic ministry, and for developing any individual's prophetic gift in corporate gatherings and planned group ministry. It's not necessary for individual ministry settings, but there is never anything wrong with coming prepared ahead of time in faith with printed prophecy. However, writing it down beforehand should never be a requirement. Ask and trust the Spirit to help gifted individuals step out in faith.

As long as it's submitted and deemed to be from the Spirit, it can be just as powerful as anything given spontaneously. However, as in all things related to the Holy Spirit, once we initiate this approach, we should expect the Holy Spirit to take certain people to new heights of faith in different methods and where He wants to go from that point.

Printed Quick Notes:
- The word received is written down on paper
- It can be a prompted or paraphrased prophecy received in prayer
- Typically read verbatim or as compiled thoughts while sharing
- Could be a picture prophecy with an interpretation and application
- Writing it down serves the leader(s) weighing the word
- It serves the speaker in helping them stay on point when sharing
- An excellent starting point in corporate and small group prophetic ministry

5. *"Praise" prophecy (song, tongue/interpretation song, poetry; Ex. 15:20-21)*

"Praise" prophecy is when the Holy Spirit uses singing or poetry to communicate a message. During worship or times of ministry there are those the Lord stirs to present their prophetic ministry in song. This is a powerful manifestation of God's grace when it's done under the anointing of the Spirit. It isn't required that the person is a gifted singer or musician; as in all things prophetic, obedience is primary. I have sung prophetic songs before, even though I am not musically inclined whatsoever. There are times when the Holy Spirit wishes to share a specific manifestation of His presence in this manner, and for those who are prompted it can be a real test of faith. If there is an instrument involved, the musician must locate the proper key and chord progression, and then allow the Holy Spirit to string the words together as they play. If the singer is not the musician, then they must work together in the Spirit to deliver the music and lyrics. In either case, the anointed result is powerful.

In the case of poetry, it's yet another powerful expression of the message He intends to encourage His Church. The length and nature of the message is at the Spirit's direction, and the individual should read the poem in faith of the Spirit's unction.

Praise Quick Notes:
- A prophetic song stirred in the heart of the messenger
- As in prompted prophecy, there may only be a direction, a few sentences, and a key
- The talent of the singer isn't what's important; it's the faith of the singer
- A written poem, prose, or rhyming verse may be shared as well

6. *"Prop/Performance" prophecy (Acts 21:11)*

In Acts 21:11, a prophet named Agabus, prophesying over Paul, borrowed his belt to bind his own feet and hands to illustrate what would happen to Paul when he went to Jerusalem.

The use of props, or physical objects, to emphasize a prophetic point symbolically was a relatively common Old Testament practice. Its continuation into the New Testament states that God will use anything to express His message. On multiple occasions I have been led of the Lord to use physical objects in a prophetic message to people. Remember, though, that any prophetic message, whether it includes a prop or not, is still subject to the test of Scripture, assessment by other prophets, and the witness of the recipient's spirit. There is no exemption from authority when there is a symbol used. In fact, it should be more carefully evaluated because of the unfortunate tendency we have toward the "sensational" in ministry.

Some ministers can take something very encouraging, add unhelpful gestures or props, and "make a show" of it that turns a "Spirit-led" ministry moment into a "flesh-flawed" farce. There is an ambition in the heart of a man that isn't always willing to let the Spirit receive all the glory during a ministry moment. This doesn't mean God will never do anything dramatic. However, while we remain open to whatever God wants to do, we remain vigilant to guard against the error of self-promotion in ministry.

It should have no other impact on the event where it's delivered than to invite the recipient(s) to draw closer to God in affection for God. The Holy Spirit doesn't need or expect anything else from us but faith, worship, and the glory to be returned to God.

Prop/Performance Quick Notes:
- Using props as the primary focus point of a prophetic message
- Symbolic gestures made or actions taken while prophesying
- Steps of faith and obedience as directed by the Spirit

7. "Prayer" prophecy (1 Tim. 4:14)

This is a prayer that can include words of knowledge, wisdom, and prophetic encouragements as the Spirit leads. The speaker may begin with their own thoughts, but during their prayer, the Spirit may begin impressing insights about the person being ministered to. These will come in sentences or pieces of information that can be prayed as needs lifted to the Lord, shared as impressions, or prayed as faith-filled opportunities for God to show Himself powerful on their behalf. It allows prophetic insights to be submitted conversationally and without fanfare, so the speaker can develop confidence in their hearing God, and the recipient can provide feedback following what was shared.

There can also be an impartation during prayer about gifts and a release of those gifts to those having hands laid on them (1 Tim. 4:14). If faith is the fuel of gift ministry from the Holy Spirit, the engine is prayer. We must be committed to coming prayerfully before the Lord whenever and wherever we sense His Spirit prompting us. Through prayer, not only are our hearts lifted out of their temporal struggle, but also we are reminded through prayer prophecy of His steadfast love and mercy securing this future and the eternal one to come. We must open our hearts and welcome His interruptions of our prayers with His presence and provision through prophetic ministry.

Prayer Quick Notes:
- A uniquely anointed prayer with specific requests coming from Spirit
- You no longer feel you are the one speaking in prayer
- Important to keep in step with Spirit; don't add any additional words
- Review content that was prophetic if it included a strong emotional response
- Get feedback about what was heard and sensed from what was prayed
- Give God all the glory

8. "Partner" prophecy (Acts 15:32)

Ministry that occurs in a team setting with a minimum of two prophetically gifted members will see uncanny complimentary ministry occurring. While we prophesy "in part," two members' "parts" may fit like jigsaw puzzle pieces through a ministry moment. It's not uncommon in this method to hear one member stop mid-sentence and the other member finish their thought. One may see a picture with many objects, while the other will see words written on the objects and receive the interpretation. One may get a word of knowledge, while the other has the prophecy about that word. Regardless of the nature of the pairing, the anointing of the Holy Spirit has fallen in such a way that links these members into an agreement that is clearly supernatural to all who are watching it play out.

Partner prophecy is the model for two-person team prophetic ministry, and it should be an expected outpouring in the anointing of the Spirit. Partners should champion each other's growth in Christ, care for each other's soul, family and relationships, and character.

Partner Quick Notes:
- When you receive part of word that you know another has the rest, or your get the second part to share
- Be faithful to only share the part you received, and wait on the Holy Spirit
- More will come when the other person shares what they see
- One person can give both parts of the word; it doesn't have to be both

9. "Preaching" prophecy (Acts 2:14-39)

In many evangelical circles, there is a common belief that pastors are the New Testament "prophets" of our day, sharing their gift through preaching and teaching. While I esteem preaching and teaching as the preeminent method God has chosen for the word of God to go forth in the world, I don't share this opinion regarding the prophetic. The belief that preachers are the ones who "prophesy" stems from the desire to smooth over some of the more difficult, unclear aspects of the boundaries of

New Testament prophecy in the church. The "prophecy is only preaching" argument falls apart very quickly when the Apostle Paul speaks of how many prophets should speak during the order or service in First Corinthians 14:29 (two or three). Couple that with the references to predictive prophecies from Agabus (Acts 11:27, 21:11), encouraging words from Judas and Silas (Acts 15:32), and the unity of prophets and teachers (Acts 13:1-3—two distinct groups mentioned together), and there appears a stand-alone ministry that has its own value to the Bride of Christ beyond preaching.

While preaching is not prophecy, it can include moments when the pastor-teacher will be overcome by the Holy Spirit and share prophetically mid-message. It could be a particularly anointed exhortation, faith-filled encouragement, word of knowledge, word of wisdom, or even a prompted prophecy. I have observed just about every method of prophecy discussed so far during a preached message. There is a sense that the pastor was stirred in a unique way from His normal teaching flow. They will often acknowledge it while it's happening or shortly after and at times even wonder who they were speaking to because it was such strong tangential message added to their talk. As a prophet, it's actually very enjoyable to see a pastor step out in faith like this, allowing the Holy Spirit to take their prepared message and infuse it with Himself. Although I believe the Holy Spirit will anoint the preacher each time he speaks, I don't believe a prophetic unction falls equally strong in every message. I would venture most pastors would agree that it isn't the same each time, but when the Spirit does come, they cannot mistake the sense of urgency, increased boldness, increased faith, and volume that accompanies the emphatic expression of the Holy Spirit to His people.

We, as the Church Body, need to pray fervently for our pastors, that the Holy Spirit would build their faith for more and more of His gracious intervention in their ministry messages. Pray that they would willingly welcome His prophetic utterance to build up the Body of Christ, and in doing so, would open their hearts to the Spirit's work of gifts through their congregations.

Preaching Quick Notes:
- Particularly anointed and specific segments of a message that flow
- These can be tracked by a heightened sense of the Spirit's presence
- The content has timely significance to the present body of believers
- It carries more than an informational anointing; there is a transformational aspect
- The pastor/teacher is typically "off his notes" in this moment and he knows it
- It won't be the entire message, but there will be moments of impartation

10. "Pastoral" prophecy (1 Tim 4:14)

This is a very common method used by pastors when they prophesy. God taps into their gift of compassion, wisdom, and care for His people and anoints them to share timely and inspiring words of hope. I call these ministry moments "pastoral" prophecy. There is a distinct outpouring of graciousness in their words, hope in the message, and faith for the future. This is typically an exhorting ministry moment that could even include a point or two shared in succession like a teaching. It will carry the anointing of the more mysterious gift of the "word of wisdom," and it is often very powerful.

1 Timothy 4 begins with a prophecy by Paul, "The Spirit expressly says..." and continues with exhortations and prophetic encouragements. This is what a pastoral prophetic word might look and sound like.

Pastors usually know the most about the people in their congregation, and in some cases they know secret things that are uncomfortable. When the Spirit uses them prophetically, there always appears to be a particular anointing for encouragement, edification or comfort that arises from their paraphrased prophecy. Their significant prior knowledge of the needs and circumstances of the people make discernment of prophetic utterance more difficult in terms of "unknown" elements, but that pre-knowledge makes them most qualified to encourage and comfort the church as the agent of God who sees the faults of people and is used to reminding them of God's hope and faithfulness in spite of it. This is a unique privilege of connection that only pastors caring for the flock will enjoy, and something the people understand and deeply appreciate.

Their prophetic ministry may not always be precise and concise, but no one seems to care because of the genuine compassion and concern being expressed in the sharing. As a prophet, I see this shepherding ministry, mixed with the authority they've been given, being uniquely anointed in that moment to share God's love for His people. Take your time, pastor; speak from your heart what you sense the Spirit is showing you. We need to hear what our compassionate God is saying through you by His Spirit.

Additional prophetic delivery methods are very common in all ministry contexts, but especially in team prophetic ministry.

Pastoral Quick Notes:
- Conversationally compassionate word given by a pastor or someone pastoral
- Primarily exhorting and encouraging
- Very close relative of the word of wisdom
- Usually anointed and filled with grace
- Shared in third-person, usually passionately; can resemble mini-teaching
- A lot of good ideas and principles with anointing; more like word of wisdom
- Could be corrective or directive

11. "Predictive" prophecy (Acts 11:28)

There is a faith-building dynamic when prophetic people are together. This is one of the most helpful benefits of team ministry. The boldness to step out a little further in faith through the Spirit is very real when there is this kind of saint-support present. This can lead to more types of "predictive" prophecy being included in ministry moments. This is more than "forth-telling" a message we sense God bringing spontaneously to mind; this includes an element of "fore-telling."

The DNA of prophetic ministry is built on speaking of the future we have been afforded through Christ and His finished work in our lives. We should expect an element of prediction in true prophetic ministry that flows from faith. We shouldn't seek to be sensational in our claims about the future in other's lives, but we shouldn't be partial cessationists either. By "partial cessationists," I mean an unwillingness to venture prophetically beyond the present in people's lives.

Predictive Quick Notes:
- Relatively common in terms of general blessing and provision
- Less common in specific dates, times, and outcomes
- Needs to be accountable and followed-up on at a later date
- Best to write it down for the person or record it for transcription later
- Encourage patience and trust in God between parts of the word that are clearly for now and what may be coming

12. "Pearls" prophecy (Acts 15:32, 21:11)

There is an expression of prophetic ministry that I have observed on multiple occasions in team settings I call "pearls" prophecy. Pearls are often associated with wisdom, knowledge, and brief statements. The Holy Spirit may direct a prophetic team to transition to sharing very short words with people. They may include a word of knowledge, wisdom, confirmation, affirmation, or prediction. These five contexts aren't exhaustive of the "pearls" prophecy method, but they speak to the revelatory nature of the gift operating in the ministry moment. There are often encouraging sound-bites about God's love, encouragement, and comfort to people during this time, but there is usually a growing faith for specificity, brevity, and clarity.

This type of ministry requires just as much faith and discipline as more involved methods, simply because it requires us to only speak what's "hot, and then hush." This is the very definition of "precise and concise." This doesn't mean we are unwilling to pause if the Holy Spirit directs us to drill deeper, but this method of ministry allows for an increased volume of ministry to occur over larger groups of people.

If a team splits up to pray for people, this is another way to get to as many people as possible. But, when working together over a group, this method is very effective in allowing multiple people to speak and to get ministered to, without getting stalled by miscues (see below).

Everything shared should have a clear point and purpose, and should not be an incomplete thought or revelation without interpretation. This may mean that one member may share a revelation and another has the interpretation or clarity of the picture. This speaks of partner prophecy, covered above, but the team element of pearls prophecy allows for a broader expression and encouragement of the prophetic in the ministry moments.

Pearls Quick Notes:
- This occurs during ministry to a group
- Usually short snippets shared quickly with great anointing
- Words of knowledge
- Words of wisdom
- Clarity, brevity, and specificity are key elements of this ministry

13. "Parable" prophecy (2 Samuel 2:1-14)

When God wanted to get David's attention, He sent Nathan the prophet to tell a story about a man who had taken advantage of another. When David's ire had been raised, the prophet used this moment to draw near to David's exposed and vulnerable emotional state, bringing the convicting line, "You are the man." David was cut to the heart by the prophet's method. There is no reason given why Nathan didn't just come out and say why he was there, but based on David's response it's possible that David would not have been so receptive to a direct confrontation.

When someone is struggling, experiencing challenges, or proud, sometimes a prophetic message delivered through a non-threatening medium, such as a story or example, can be a very compassionate, convincing, and convicting approach. The Bible says that God's kindness leads us to repentance and we can all benefit from His kind and gentle confrontation through metaphors, stories, or examples that are anointed by the Holy Spirit to reveal the secrets of our hearts.

This should not be forced or contrived as a method to confront sin, but rather, like all prophetic ministry, trust the Holy Spirit to not only give the message, but also to direct the best method of delivery. It's this obedience to the proper delivery that creates the forum for true anointing and repentance to occur.

Parables Quick Notes:
- A prophetic message delivered in story form
- Nathan prophesied this way over David
- Jesus spoke in parables to the disciples
- Parable messages will typically have an interpretation or point made at the end

14. "Presbytery" prophecy (1 Tim. 4:14)

This is typically a planned prophetic ministry opportunity organized for the purpose of seeing what God might have to say about specifically selected people in a fellowship. These are men and women the local church elders recognize for their proven character, gifting, faithfulness, and readiness for expanded ministry opportunities. Timothy was the recipient of this type of ministry when Paul laid hands on him with the rest of the elders and imparted gifts into him for the ministry God was calling Him to. Acts 13 speaks of prophets and teachers coming together in prayer for the mission of the Church, resulting in the call of Paul and Barnabas for their ministry. This ministry method will incorporate just about every method of prophecy we've discussed and more. This is a demonstration of the church's faith and support of those gifted and called within the church. Developing ministers desperately need encouragement from the body to grow their faith, and this is a practical and powerful means of grace for that expression.

"Presbytery" prophecy is the Holy Spirit's way of coming alongside the elders and strengthening their resolve to move ministry forward in people's lives. This should also be a faith-building ministry for the congregation as they rejoice to see and hear the Holy Spirit raise those who've been obedient and faithful. This should encourage many to want that same ministry and confirmation in their own lives. This is why elders should be continually praying and seeking candidates to bring before the church, not for ordination but for elevation in their faith and gifts.

It's my prayer that faith will rise again for presbytery prophecy in the church as a means of grace for identification and expansion of the gifts that can mature the Bride for our Savior's return.

Presbytery Quick Notes:
- Team ministry over an individual or group of people
- Usually administrated by one or two people gifted to do so
- Involves many forms of prophetic ministry and gifts
- Impartation and activation of candidate leaders is a significant part of ministry

15. "Proxy" prophecy (Acts 15:27-28)

In the development of team ministry, we have experienced the power of "proxy" prophecy. This occurs when a member of the prophetic team cannot be present to minister at a particular event but will pray and see what God might have for the team or people being prayed for. The prophetic team will take what is submitted with them to the event and share it as from the Holy Spirit. This allows even the absent member of the team to continue to be a part of the team despite being absent. It encourages them to always be ready and in faith for what God might use them to do, even if they are providentially hindered from going to the event.

Proxy prophecy understands team ministry, humility, and whose glory this entire ministry is for. It doesn't care who gets the credit, just as long as God gets the glory and the Church is built up.

Proxy Quick Notes:
- A word we receive for another that is given by another
- Write it down, walk away, and pray
- God is sovereign; He doesn't need us, but He includes us even when absent
- Significance is continuing faith to be used even when absent
- Not that we are so significant that the word can't happen if we aren't present

Appendix B

Prophetic Ministry Miscues

Sometimes, a prophecy... isn't.

Miscues happen, and properly managing ministry when enthusiastic people shared inappropriately, or are flat wrong, is the difference between building up an individual and quashing the Spirit.

Pastors, elders, or the mature prophetic person on the team needs to administrate the gifts. There should be at least one leader (gifted prophet or pastor) who provides oversight and timing for the team direction during ministry. This means He listens to all the words the team is sensing, and He is allowing the Holy Spirit to direct his decisions about what should be shared when, and whether it should be shared at all. What is being received and shared needs to be weighed as to whether it's prophetic or just a positive confirmation of what God is doing in general. The gift of discernment, faith, administration, leadership, and prophecy are all operating in that person simultaneously to assist the team in effectively ministering to the people.

Further, these leaders have the responsibility to help prophetic people develop in their gifts, through gentle admonishment and teaching.

Common Miscues To Address Include:

1. "Pasta" prophecy

With reference to prophetic team ministry, "pasta" prophecy is taken from the old adage, "let's throw the pasta at the wall and see what sticks." In other words, there are people "stepping out in faith" with a lot to share for others, but there isn't clarity about the direction taken for a person or group.

Pasta Quick Notes:
- Usually occurs in team ministry, presbytery, or group prayer prophecy

- There are multiple words shared that don't really have the same direction
- There is a need to discern the prophetic from the merely positive

2. "Parrot" prophecy

In a team ministry setting, it's extremely common to experience "parrot" prophecy. This usually occurs when a genuine prophetic word is given, and an inexperienced person follows up with the same points of the original word. They may feel it's different for two reasons. First, it could be something they saw before the other word was shared, so they feel the need to validate it with what they saw. Second, they might know something about the person prophesied over and wishes to affirm what was prophesied.

Parrot Quick Notes:
- When a person restates a previously given prophetic word
- This typically occurs in a group ministry setting
- Might be slightly different words, but the essence is the same

3. "Prolonged" prophecy

Prompted first-person prophecy is powerful and effective, so not only must we learn to surrender our voice and right to participate in the outpouring's effects on us, but also we must be vigilant in brevity. There are many times when I've heard individuals begin a highly anointed word only to move into adding interpretive exhortations to the ministry moment. Hold fast to those two simple words: *precise* and *concise*. We must be accurate and brief, that is "speak what's hot, then hush." Say only what is given without commentary or embellishment.

In "prolonged" prophecy, the speaker may speak too long and not realize it. This particularly afflicts prompted prophecy. Precise and concise is easier said than done, and it's easy to miss by the prophet in the moment.

Prolonged Quick Notes:
- Just speaking too much
- Need to understand the concept of precise and concise

4. "Partial" prophecy

The opposite number of "prolonged" is "partial." Partial prophecy is missing the hook. The hook is the central theme of the prophetic word that is intended to be confirming, affirming, or proclaimed to the hearer(s). It is given by the Holy Spirit and is a strong indication it is to be shared. In its absence, don't share. The hook may be confirmation, affirmation, or proclamation of what God has done, is doing, or will do. It could be a simple sentence, a picture with a clear interpretive statement, or series of words driving toward a powerful declaration of God's faithfulness to them. If the speaker doesn't receive any more than a partial sentence or series of words that don't seem to have any connection to a point, the ministry moment will be confusing. Sometimes that means the speaker just missed the interpretation and timing of the word, or it was given to the wrong person.

Many times, it can also mean that the speaker didn't wait on the Lord long enough to receive an interpretation. There must be a hook in our hearts before we share. A clear witness of direction. A reasonable clarity of what we are sharing. We may not have any idea what it means to them or how it may apply, but it should at least be a complete thought in our minds.

Partial Quick Notes:
- Only get a portion of the word given
- Perforated because has a lot of holes in it

5. "Pinwheel" prophecy

This ministry miscue is common when we don't get a clear interpretation of something we are sensing. This can happen after receiving a picture that has no clear application, or we begin speaking about what we thought the Holy Spirit was revealing, but while the words are often very encouraging and comforting, it soon becomes evident that we aren't really saying anything particularly prophetic. What typically happens is that we can be so stirred by something we are feeling for someone or in response to something someone else said to them that we start down a direction and lose our place. This leads to trying to recover with all kinds of don't-hear-what-I'm-not-saying adjustments, positioning points, and caveats.

It's much better to humbly bow out and reconnect with the Spirit and team than to force a bad position hoping someone on the team will get inspired and bail you out. Usually when the pinwheel is spinning, the team is also confused.

We must take each ministry moment as its own unique opportunity to trust the Holy Spirit for discernment. We must never assume that what worked in one moment will work in the next with Him. We must have the discipline, regardless of how awkward it might appear to others, to pause and confirm what we are getting before proceeding.

Pinwheel Quick Notes:
- Prophecy without a point of focus
- Lots of colorful words

6. *"Profiling" prophecy*

Another miscue common to those new to this ministry is exemplified by the Prophet Samuel's struggle with "profiling" when prophesying the next King. When he saw Jesse's firstborn son and saw his stature and look, he said, "Surely the Lord's anointed is before me" (1 Samuel 16:6). He was corrected by God to keep searching because the Lord looks on the heart of a man. We are all susceptible to visual profiling in the prophetic ministry, not just in thinking a well-appointed person is of sterling character, but in assuming a poorly dressed person is of low character.

If, in our human hearts, we check a prophecy because we

think, "Surely, God, this person can't be..." or "This prophecy must be for someone else..." then we must instead trust the Holy Spirit's prompt. Take care also for outward displays of tears, stoic responses, or any other external response as acceptance or rejection of a word. God knows the heart and trusting His Spirit's leading remains our best affirmation.

Profiling Quick Notes:
- Like Samuel with Jesse's firstborn, we see external cues rather than God's cues
- We draw our inspiration from the person's tears or response
- We know something about the situation and we speak from our experience

7. "Panoramic" prophecy

The final miscue that falls in the "teachable moments" category is "panoramic" prophecy. This is pinwheel prophecy but with a picture or vision. It's easy to believe a received picture should be the focus of sharing. Maybe yes, maybe no, but if the message goes into painstaking detail of every facet and movement of the picture and God's pointed message is delayed or omitted, the recipient will become confused or impatient (if the prophet is missing the Holy Spirit's stirring, it isn't a surprise if the recipient doesn't either). This is a sign of a person putting more stock in their imagination than the Spirit's word to the person(s). It's understandable that seeing something wonderful is so captivating that it replaces the meaning, but the tendency must be corrected. There is nothing wrong with a detailed vision; it really comes down to being precise and concise in relating the picture and stressing the interpretation. If the picture becomes more important, then the anointing will be lost.

Panoramic Quick Notes:
- A word with a picture described for so long that the anointing picked up and left for home

- A substantial preoccupation with the picture scene and little on what it means
- A lot of description about the picture and what you see; very little interpretation
- The application can suffer badly as well

Appendix C

Prophetic Ministry Misrepresentations

Teachable moments are for miscues that show a lack of knowledge or awareness. Misrepresentations of character and harm may require attention, follow-up, and correction.

Misrepresentations To Address Include:

1. "Parking Lot" prophecy

"Parking lot" prophecy gets its name from the one-on-one, unchecked prophetic sharing in a private or individual setting (like getting bushwhacked in the parking lot by someone who feels they must share a word with you). There is often nothing wrong with one-on-one sharing, but the motivation behind the individual approach isn't necessarily privacy but possibly getting around authority. This kind of "ministry" is more prevalent than may be realized.

If the prophetic person believes the leadership doesn't trust him, the prophetic person may circumvent the protocols of submission, partnership, and team and deliver their message on the side. Such people feel they are obeying God in sharing, but because there are unresolved relational issues with leadership, they don't include leadership.

Pastors will get wind of this character flaw when they are forced to do damage control in counseling sessions. It's a difficult place for a pastor to plead ignorance of something they should know about. The prophetic person may sense no obligation to the pastor, but the pastor has an obligation to care for the members who are potentially confused or harmed by the word.

This isn't obedience, its presumption. Proverbs 29:11 says "A fool gives full vent to his spirit, but a wise man quietly holds it back."

Maturity is required in discerning what is shared outside

of the normal contexts of prophetic ministry. When sharing without a leader present or a pastor's knowledge, the prophetic person must search his or her heart for the purpose in cutting out the pastor. Further, the prophetic person must then take on the burden of consequences in influencing actions or responses of the hearer.

> *Parking Lot Quick Notes:*
> - Prophecies consistently shared outside the realm of accountability or submission
> - Rarely is anyone but the speaker and recipient present when word is shared
> - Message tends to have predictive, directive, or corrective elements
> - Usually causes anxiety on the part of the recipient because of the message's nature
> - There may be elements of accuracy, but this subversive approach drains credibility
> - May include slanderous, critical, or disloyal tones toward leadership
> - Tend to originate from people not fully committed to the Church

2. *"Proud" prophecy*

"Proud" prophecy is an element in all the corrective miscues, but here there is a "lone ranger" mentality. They have little to no interest in working on a team beyond getting their chance to be used up front. When it comes to feedback, adjustment, reliability, deference to authority, humbly responding to repositioning, timing, or manner of delivery, they bristle and push back.

Most of the time this will happen in the absence of a true relationship between the members outside of the ministry. It's important that no one be active in team ministry that doesn't have a strong relationship with multiple members of the team. If relationships are limited, then that person's opportunity should be limited as well. This is not because they aren't gifted; they just haven't demonstrated that they are willing to be a team player when things don't go as they think they should.

Proud Quick Notes:
- Man-centered, self-serving, puffed up words that focus on delivery, not content
- Performance enhanced inflection to sound prophetic
- Lacks the fruit of the Spirit in delivery; can be raw or harsh in tone
- Preoccupation with drawing attention to anointing and how God is using them

3. *"Pathetic" prophecy*

"Pathetic" prophecy is when someone seeks to appear prophetic and spiritual when they are sharing things that not only aren't prophetic, but also aren't even consistent with Scripture.

Such a person needs to be addressed as quickly and gently as possible, in the moment.

Sadly, the person sharing this way may have no idea that they missed the mark—perhaps through lack of biblical knowledge or just a genuine desire to be helpful. This is why compassion must carry the day in our work with them. They must be gently made to see what the responsibility of the prophetic is and how it is administrated. Otherwise, in the absence of that clarity, it just appears to be a New Age psychic fair that allows anyone to share what they feel or perceive in their own imaginations.

Pathetic Quick Notes:
- Lacks anointing, and actually causes anxiety because it's delivered so poorly
- Inaccurate and doesn't witness with the spirit
- Continuing to question and qualify after initial query is wrong
- Clearly not scripturally based or sound

4. "Presumptuous" prophecy

The big brother to "pathetic" prophecy is "presumptuous" prophecy. The unresponsive and self-serving attitude of a minister ramps it up to presumptuous level. Here again, a measure of what is seen may be valid and from God, but the individual's predisposition to resist authority, humility, or team ministry invalidates what's being shared.

This type of mistake is generally felt more internally between the team members in the ministry moments and should be quickly addressed, privately and gently.

Harshness is never the appropriate reaction to these sinful failures. We as prophetic ministers are all susceptible to the very same failures at different moments, or have done so before, so we should treat the failing minister as we would want to be treated, with Christ's love and patience. If they are responsive, then God has built our relationship closer; if not, He has protected the Body of Christ from something unhelpful.

Whenever corrective ministry is required, the fruit of the Spirit must be evident in the correcting agent. The goal is always caring for the heart of the saint, not the protection of our reputation or ministry. God is able to overcome failure when godly leadership is present. This is why we need to pray that God will develop senior prophetic ministry members in our midst so that we can care for the gift's growth in the local church in a purposeful God honoring way.

Presumptuous Quick Notes:
- Using prophetic concepts heard elsewhere to share in a prophetic manner
- Teaching or correcting in a prophetic manner
- Sharing positive, upbeat outcomes to enhance good feelings about the person sharing
- Sharing excessive interpretive insight or application
- Wishful thoughts for good things shared as prophetic
- The longer first-person words last they become increasingly less reliable

Glossary

This set of definitions is intended to diminish confusion regarding certain terms I use to describe contexts and content in the prophetic ministry to the Church. It's my hope that this glossary increases clarity while providing a more robust picture of the teaching concepts being presented.

Care/Small Group: Groups of church members gathering for Bible study, fellowship, prayer, and ministry. It can be a meeting in the church building or in members' homes, and it is typically led by a leadership-team-recognized member with a proven gift of leadership (not necessarily an elder or deacon) (Acts 5:42).

Corporate (Congregational) Prophetic Ministry: Any prophetic ministry shared with the gathered congregation during a regular service. This would typically be from a member or someone known to the leadership, and/or be content judged to be appropriate for edification of the Body of Christ (Acts 11:28).

Discernment of Spirits: The prompting of the Holy Spirit to understand what He is doing in a person, small group, or congregation. This also includes an awareness of any demonic activity, human spirit influence, and/or the current disposition of the human spirits present (Luke 5:22; John 1:47, 5:19; Acts 5:3-4, 16:16; 1 John 4:1-3).

Exhortation: Any encouraging, strengthening, or challenging message originating from wisdom or experience gained through the Holy Spirit but is not necessarily a direct word from God in the moment. It can be shared as an application of a Scripture, an up-building sentiment, a call to action, or even a warning. This is typically a more natural occurrence offered by faith as prompted by the Spirit for the edification of the hearer(s) (Rom. 12:6-8).

Leadership or Elder Team: Any governmental structure, or polity, that oversees the local expression of the Body of Christ including, but not limited to, pastors, elders, bishops, overseers, deacons, administrators, deacon boards, and elder boards. The word *team* is a way to globally identify the God-ordained authority in the local church across multiple denominational and doctrinal structures without elevating any particular approach or model (Titus 1:5-13; 1 Tim. 4:14; 2 Tim. 3:1-13).

The encouragement from the word *team* is intended to highlight the value of each godly leader's contribution to oversight of the local church and the wisdom it would be for the pastor(s) to create a context of reasonable plurality and input for accountability, support, and safety. Not every leader is expected to be equal in authority or position on the team, but it's incumbent on the primary leadership to create the sense of team in their humility, example, and communication.

Ministry Moment: The act of serving (especially with one's gifts) another person in the church through meeting a practical need, praying over them, or offering counsel (Acts 21:11; 1 Peter 4:10).

Ministry Team: Any group of local church members submitted to the God-ordained authority of the local leadership team, with leaders who are "first among equals" in serving the church with their various gifts (Acts 11:27, 15:32).

Ministry Time: Leadership-team-directed times of praying for church members with specific physical, spiritual, mental, or emotional needs during any corporate or small group gathering. Prayer ministry will often include laying (or placing outstretched) hands on the person(s) being prayed for (Acts 13:1-3; 1 Tim. 4:14; James 5:14).

Personal Prophecy: Any prophetic ministry from one believer to another (Acts 21:11).

Presbytery: Any team prophetic ministry where elders and/or prophets are ministering together over an individual(s), small group, or a congregation. Usually accompanied by the laying of hands (Acts 13:1-3; 1 Tim. 4:14).

Prophecy: A direct quote, picture, or vision from God to His church, brought forth through any Spirit-filled Christian who professes Jesus Christ is Lord. This is a supernatural manifestation of the Spirit (Rom. 12:6; 1 Cor. 14:3).

Prophecy should be edifying and may include Scripture verses, predictive elements, directive elements, corrective elements, conditional elements, warning elements, words of wisdom, words of knowledge, or discernment of spirits. It should also be tested against Scripture and the witness of the Holy Spirit (1 Thess. 5:19; 1 John 4:1-3).

The distinctions being made between the gifts of prophecy, word of wisdom, word of knowledge, and discerning of spirits is best applied in training prophetic people to discern the Spirit's leading in ministry. It isn't necessary to highlight these distinctions for people while providing ministry.

The Spirit will regularly intertwine their use in prophetic ministry to edify believers, so it's most important to direct people's focus to His kindness and grace being revealed to the Church, not to the mixed method of delivery.

Prophet/Prophetess: One called by Jesus Christ to serve the local church and the wider body of Christ as the Holy Spirit leads, by equipping and encouraging the saints for the work of the ministry. They do this through sharing what they believe God is saying to the Church and training others to serve with the gifts of the Spirit, especially prophecy (Acts 11:28, 21:9; 1 Cor. 12:29; Eph. 4:11).

Prophetic Team: Any group of local church members recognized and recruited by the local church leadership team to serve alongside, grow with, and be accountable to one another in the ministry of prophecy to the Body of Christ (Acts 11:27, 13:1, 15:32).

Vocal Ministry: Any believer who speaks before the congregation (small group and/or individual) with an intent to edify (1 Cor. 14:26).

Word of Knowledge*: Any message from the Holy Spirit that includes *knowledge, facts, or information* that would not be known to the speaker beforehand, or a timely instruction (*teaching*) illuminated by the Spirit from Scripture (Acts 5:3-4, 9:11-12; John 4:4).

Word of Wisdom*: Any word or message shared as an *application or directive* from the Holy Spirit for a specific situation, or a timely insight (*specific application*) illuminated by the Spirit from Scripture (Acts 9:11-12, 16:6-7).

* Since both word of knowledge and word of wisdom are listed as manifestations of the Spirit, these are supernatural expressions that occur during ministry or preaching, not naturally possessed gifts or preaching skills. There is very little explanation given about these gifts in Scripture, so these definitions are submitted with humility and a continuing openness to learn. I like how my friend and prophet, Dr. Ray Self, described it at Freedom Fellowship in 2014 the difference and relationship between these gifts: "A word of knowledge is something the Spirit reveals to us that we didn't know; the word of wisdom would be what the Spirit tells us to do with that information." For example, in Acts 9:11 Ananias learns through a word of knowledge of Saul's presence on Straight Street, and in Acts 9:12 he is then directed through a word of wisdom from the Spirit to serve him in a specific way through a vision where he lays hands on him to recover his sight.

About the Author

Darin Slack is married to his wife of twenty-five years, Lesli, and has five children, Matthew, Michael, Mark, Meaghan, and Meredith. He is a long-time member of Metro Life Church in Casselberry, FL where he serves as a commissioned Prophetic Team leader. As a bi-vocational leader who makes his living in the secular arena, he is also the President and Founder of National Football Academies, where he and his team serve young quarterbacks with training, camps, and resources that are recognized by many coaches and parents as the industry standard for skill development. More importantly, it's the biblically based message of manhood in that program that has impacted over fifty thousand young men and coaches in the football world.

Prophetic Seminars, Workshops and Conferences Available For Your Church

Darin Slack has a passion to equip local church leaders and members in God-glorifying prophetic ministry. He and members of the team look forward to serving leaders and churches in multiple ways:

Online/webinar workshops – These are trainings provided over Skype, Webex, or other online web-based resource.

Evening ministry training workshops – These are local trainings for churches who desire encouragement and assistance in developing their prophetic ministry.

1- or 2-day prophetic workshops – These are local, or extra-local, equipping and activation sessions for churches desiring assistance in prophetic ministry for their leadership and/or members.

Weekend conference seminars – These can be local, or extra-local, equipping and activation sessions like the 1-2 day workshops, but include more formal teaching and ministry.

"Darin Slack and his team of gifted ministers, trained us to walk in greater intimacy and dependence upon our God and to see the Spirit's gift of prophecy thrive in our Church. If your heart is to equip and mobilize your people in one of the biblically essential areas prescribed by God to be a healthy church, I have no greater recommendation than to bring Darin and his team in… I know this, we will never be the same… to the glory of God!"

—*Paul Cooke, Senior pastor, City Church, Athens GA*

For more information on how these events can
help your church, contact Darin Slack at:
Reclaimingprophecy@gmail.com

Need
additional
copies?

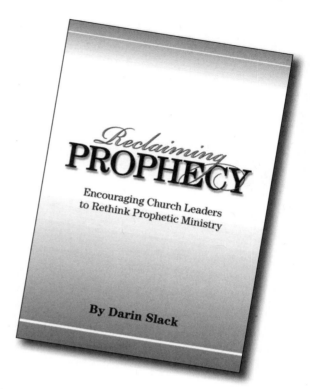

To order more copies of

contact CertaPublishing.com

☐   Order online at:
    CertaPublishing.com/ReclaimingProphecy

☐   Call 855-77-CERTA or

☐   Email Info@CertaPublishing.com